MW01181663

LEGENDS
OF THE
AlefBet

The Origins of the Alphabet

PROFESSOR MIRIAM HOFFMAN

Coral Springs, Florida
www.YiddishkaytInitiative.org
www.MiriamHoffman.com

Color Alef-Beyz letters created by artist Michoel Muchnik

The letters of the Kinstlerisher alef beys by Ben-Tsiyon Zuckerman
are from the Library of the YIVO Institute for Jewish Research

Image on page 53 courtesy of YIVO Institute for Jewish Research
(Discovered by Mendl Hoffman)

Print ISBNs: 978-0-9993365-2-6   hardcover
978-0-9993365-3-3   softcover

Proofread by Carol Killman Rosenberg • www.carolkillmanrosenberg.com
Cover and interior by Gary A. Rosenberg • www.garyarosenberg.com

Printed in the United States of America

Introduction

omewhat more than five millennia ago, a human hand first carved a written word on stone, and so initiated recorded history. Five thousand years of writing, using societally agreed upon alphabets, followed.

Where did our alphabets originate?

This happened in Sumer (3800–2000 BCE), the world's first civilization, a land made up of twenty-five city states. It had risen to dominate all of Mesopotamia. Sumer is considered the cradle of civilization, with their highly developed techniques in farming, inventory of agricultural storage facilities, wheeled transport, sailing ships, metallurgy, and oven-baked pottery. They also developed an innovative method of construction for business, stone sculpture, and engraving.

Their language was Sumerian; later on, it was replaced by Akkadian/old Babylonian, using no less than 200 words just to describe different varieties of sheep.

Sumer mythology talks of a primordial flood, of a Garden of Paradise—called Eden and the creation of the first man by a Father God who molded the man out of clay. Heaven was referred to as "Heavenly Father," while Earth was referred to as "Mother Earth." The ancients knew mathematics, square roots, and cube roots, calculating the size of a field accurately; they also knew the art of building and excavation, which eventually led to the making of a canal.

Theirs was practical medicine, not magical.

With Semitic nomads wandering along the mountains and deserts outside of the pale of Sumer, they encountered the city state of Uruk, along the Tigris and Euphrates Rivers in ancient Mesopotamia, present-day Iraq.

The capital city of Sumer was Ur Chaldea, or Ur Kashdim. The capital depended on which city was dominant in any given period of time.

Nanna-Sin was the Sumerian Moon God, the bull was sacred to Nanna-Sin, especially the Bull's Horns (see image at left) out of which sprang the first letter of our Jewish alphabet, namely Alef, representing the word *Aluf*, which in today's Israel represents general or commander.

At Uruk (Iraq)—Ishtar was the fickle Goddess of Love, Aram Naharayim were called the Two Rivers. Ur was also the birthplace of the biblical forefather of the three main world religions—Jewish, Christian, and Muslim—Abraham, also known as Avram, Avraham, and Ibrahim.

Practically all the letters of the Hebrew alphabet were related to the ancient Semitic alphabets, among them Ugaric, Akkadian, Syriac, Phoenician, Aramaic, Ethiopian, and Arabic.

Practically all the letters of the Hebrew alphabet were related to the ancient Semitic alphabets, among them Ugaric, Akkadian, Syriac, Phoenician, Aramaic, Ethiopian, and Arabic.

Babylonia was the direct successor to Sumer. Biblical scholars and historians are of the opinion that the Semitic alphabet stems from the Babylonian script. Others say that it stems from old Egyptian.

The Hebrew alphabet, with some differences, was introduced by Ezra Hasofer at the time of the Second Temple, two and a half thousand years ago, when the Jews returned from Babylonian exile. This alphabet is called Ktav Ashuri, Assyrian script.

The old Greek, Latin, and Russian/Cyrillic alphabets have roots in our Semitic alphabet.

Aram, today's Syria, is the name of a country that existed in biblical times. Its borders reached all the way to Babylonia, today's Iraq. The people of Aram were called Aramains. The language of the Aramains was Aramaic.

Aramaic was spoken three and a half thousand years ago north of Israel, Syria, Babylonia, Persia, and Armenia.

A great many Jews spoke Aramaic around fifteen hundred years ago and created a substantial body of work in that language. As a matter of fact, you can find Jews today who still speak Aramaic.

Jews spoke and created in a great many Jewish languages, which helped them survive two thousand years of exile. (All the Jewish languages were written in the Hebrew alphabet.)

Among the longest-surviving Jewish languages, not including Hebrew, Aramaic, and Ladino, is Yiddish, which is more than one thousand years old.

Jews spoke and created in a great many Jewish languages, which helped them survive two thousand years of exile.

The written laws of the time were given to us in Assyrian, which we adopted as the old Hebraic written script known as the Torah.

After the destruction of the first Temple in 586 BCE, the Jews of Israel spoke Assyrian. So Yehuda (Judah) Hanasi used to say:

> **"Of what use is it to you Jews to speak Assyrian in Israel? Why don't you speak the true Jewish language, *Lashon Kadosh*, the sacred tongue, or at least the universal language—Greek?"**

Rabbi Yosef (Joseph) used to say:

> **"Of what use is it to you Jews in Babylonia to speak Aramaic? Why don't you speak your own language, *Lashon Kadosh*? Or at least Persian?**

The Jews of that day answered:

> **"For singing—we use Greek. For army drills—we use spoken Roman. (Latin).**
>
> **For writing, we use Assyrian. And amongst ourselves, we use Lashon Kadosh (the sacred biblical tongue)."**

According to the mystic traditions of the Kabbalists, during the Middle Ages, the coming of the Messiah is dependent on our ability to calculate, through *gematria*—numerology—all the numeric value combinations of the letters of the Alef-Bet. The secrets of God's creation and the exact date of our redemption is hidden in the letters of the Torah. With the help of computers, the answer should be discovered any day now.

According to the Kabbalists, the Alef-Bet has a life of its own. The letters speak and argue amongst themselves, they exert their power, plead with God, and cause a commotion in this world and the world to come.

> The Jewish Alef-Bet is written from right to left because, in the beginning of time, letters were chiseled on stone from right to left, unlike the Greek, Cyrillic, or Latin Alphabets, which are written from left to right.

The twenty-two letters of the Alef-Bet are the fundamental building blocks of our modern culture. The mystics believed that as soon as the twenty-third letter would be discovered, Paradise would descend upon the earth, and the world order will radically change forever.

According to the Jewish tradition, God used the letters of the Alef-Bet as a blueprint and a building block for the creation of the world. God hewed large boulders out of the void. He drew them through water, stormed them through intangible air, kindled them in fire, and melted them into the twenty-two letters of our Alef-Bet. And from that moment on, the letters adorned the Crown of the Almighty.

In this book we explore the etymology, evolution, and folklore of each of those letters.

Table of Alphabets

The sounds of the letters in Arabic, Hebrew, Greek, Russian, and German are shown in parentheses

ENGLISH	ARABIC		HEBREW		GREEK			RUSSIAN		GERMAN	
Upper and Lower Case					Print and Script			Upper and Lower Case		Upper and Lower Case	
A a	ا	Alif *1*	א Aleph *4*		A α	Alpha	(ä)	А а	(ä)	𝔄 𝔞	(ä)
B b	ﺑ ﺒ ﺐ	Be (b)	ב Beth	(b)	B β	Beta	(b)	Б б	(b)	𝔄̈ ä	(e) *5*
C c	ﺗ ﺘ ﺖ	Te (t)	ב Veth	(v) *5*	Γ γ	Gamma	(g)	В в	(v)	𝔅 𝔟	(b)
D d	ﺛ ﺜ ﺚ	Se (th)	ג Gimel	(g)	Δ δ	Delta	(d)	Г г	(g)	ℭ 𝔠	(k, ts, s)
E e	ﺟ ﺠ ﺞ	Jim (j) *2*	ד Daleth	(d)	E ε	Epsilon	(e)	Д д	(d)	𝔠𝔥 𝔠𝔥	(H, kh)
F f	ﺣ ﺤ ﺢ	He (h) *2*	ה Heh	(h)	Z ζ	Zeta	(z)	Е е	(ye)	𝔇 𝔡	(d)
G g	ﺧ ﺨ ﺦ	Khe (kh) *2*	ו Vav	(v)	H η	Eta	(ā)	Ж ж	(zh)	𝔈 𝔢	(e, ā)
H h	ﺩ	Dal (d)	ז Zayin	(z)	Θ θ	Theta	(th)	З з	(z)	𝔉 𝔣	(f)
I i	ﺫ	Zal (*th*)	ח Kheth	(kh)	I ι	Iota	(ē)	И и	(i, ē)	𝔊 𝔤	(g, kh)
J j	ﺭ	Re (r)	ט Teth	(t)	K κ	Kappa	(k)	Й й	(ē) *7*	𝔥 𝔥	(h)
K k	ﺯ	Ze (z)	י Yod	(y)	Λ λ	Lambda	(l)	К к	(k)	𝔍 𝔦	(i, ē)
L l	ﺳ ﺴ ﺲ	Sin (s) *2*	כך Kaph	(k) *6*	M μ	Mu	(m)	Л л	(l)	𝔍 𝔧	(y)
M m	ﺷ ﺸ ﺶ	Shin (sh) *2*	כך Khaph	(kh) *5, 6*	N ν	Nu	(n)	М м	(m)	𝔎 𝔨	(k)
N n	ﺻ ﺼ ﺺ	Sad (s) *2*	ל Lamedh	(l)	Ξ ξ	Xi	(ks)	Н н	(n)	𝔏 𝔩	(l)
O o	ﺿ ﻀ ﺾ	Dad (*th*) *2*	מם Mem	(m) *6*	O ο	Omicron	(o)	О о	(ô, o)	𝔐 𝔪	(m)
P p	ﻃ	Ta (t)	נן Nun	(n) *6*	Π π	Pi	(p)	П п	(p)	𝔑 𝔫	(n)
Q q	ﻇ	Za (z)	ס Samekh	(s)	P ρ	Rho	(r)	Р р	(r)	𝔒 𝔬	(ō, ô)
R r	ﻋ ﻌ ﻊ	Ain *2, 3*	ע Ayin *4*		Σ σ ς	Sigma	(s) *6*	С с	(s)	𝔒̈ ö	(ö) *5*
S s	ﻏ ﻐ ﻎ	Ghain (kh) *2*	פ Peh	(p)	T τ	Tau	(t)	Т т	(t)	𝔓 𝔭	(p)
T t	ﻓ ﻔ ﻒ	Fe (f) *2*	פף Feh	(f) *5, 6*	Υ υ	Upsilon	(ü, ōō)	У у	(ōō)	𝔔(u)q(u)	(kv)
U u	ﻗ ﻘ ﻖ	Qaf (kä) *2*	צץ Tsadi	(ts) *6*	Φ φ	Phi	(f)	Ф ф	(f)	𝔑 𝔯	(r)
V v	ﻛ ﻜ ﻚ	Kef (k) *2*	ק Koph	(k)	X χ	Chi	(H)	Х х	(kh)	𝔖 𝔰	(s, z) *6*
W w	ﻟ ﻠ ﻞ	Lam (l) *2*	ר Resh	(r)	Ψ ψ	Psi	(ps)	Ц ц	(ts)	𝔖𝔠𝔥 𝔰𝔠𝔥	(sh)
X x	ﻣ ﻤ ﻢ	Mim (m) *2*	שׁ Shin	(sh)	Ω ω	Omega	(ō)	Ч ч	(ch)	𝔗 𝔱	(t)
Y y	ﻧ ﻨ ﻦ	Nun (n) *2*	שׂ Sin	(s) *5*				Ш ш	(sh)	𝔘 𝔲	(ōō)
Z z	ﻫ	He (h)	ת Tav	(t)				Щ щ	(shch)	𝔘̈ ü	(ü) *5*
	ﻭ	Waw (w)	ת Thav	(th, s) *5*				Ъ ъ	*8*	𝔙 𝔳	(f)
	ﻳ	Ye (y) *6*						Ы ы	(ē)	𝔚 𝔴	(v)
								Ь ь	*9*	𝔛 𝔵	(ks)
								Э э	(e)	𝔜 𝔶	(ē, ü)
								Ю ю	(u)	𝔷 𝔷	(ts)
								Я я	(yä)		

Diacritical Marks used with Hebrew Characters

⟋	(ô, ŏ)	¨	(ā)	:	(silent)
−	(ä)	⦙	(e)	⦙·	(ōō)
		·	(i, ē)		

NOTES

1. *A neutral letter, silent in the middle of words, but represented by ('), indicating the glottal stop, when used at the beginning of a word.*
2. *The first form is used at the beginning of a word; the second, in the middle; the third, at the end.*
3. *A neutral letter represented by ('), indicating rough breathing, when used at the beginning of a word.*
4. *A neutral letter, either silent or sounded according to the accompanying diacritical mark.*
5. *A variant of the preceding character, not counted in the alphabet.*
6. *The final form is used only as the last letter of a word and (in German) of some syllables.*
7. *Used only as the second vowel in a diphthong.*
8. *Indicates nonpalatalization of a preceding consonant.*
9. *Indicates palatalization of a preceding consonant.*

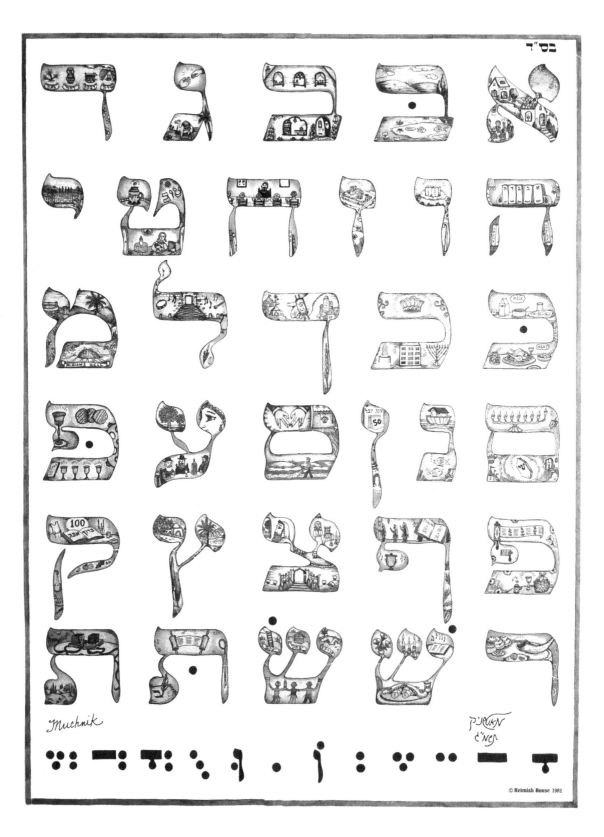

בס"ד

Muchnik

נאכלַיין
ניסעל

© Heimish House 1982

א Alef

א Alef

Ah Sound, Numeric Value of 1

Proto-Canaanite • 1500 BCE

Sumerian—Aluf	Phoenician—Alef
Akkadian—Alpu	Greek—Alpha
Arabic—Alif	English—Ay

Alef is the first letter of the Hebrew alphabet. The Alef represents balance.

The first representation of the Alef is an ancient Phoenician figure of the letter depicting the horns of a bull, representing a yoke or a burden, as well as an instrument of agriculture.

According to folklore, when God was about to create the world by His word alone, the twenty-two letters descended from His Crown, where they were engraved with a pen of flaming fire. They surrounded the Holy One, Blessed Be He, and one after the other pleaded with Him:

"Create the world with me!"

Legend has it that when God's decision to create the world with the second letter of the Alef-Bet—Bet: *Breyshit* (in the beginning)—it became known throughout His domain that the Alef was devastated. She stood all alone bewailing her fate.

Suddenly the voice of the Creator interrupted her grief:

"Alef! Why are you so quiet?"

To which the Alef replied:

"Lord of the Universe! I have no courage to speak up, after all, mine is the lowest numeric value—I am only one."

And to the letter Alef, God said:

"You are One, I am One and the Torah is One. Not to worry, I will put you at the head of the Alef-Bet, you will be the 'Crown' among the letters. Remember, the Torah will be given through all the letters of the Alef-Bet to my people Israel on Mt. Sinai."

And, according to tradition, the Almighty himself came down to Mt. Sinai to give the Jews the Ten Commandments and the Torah.

The Ten Commandments starts with the sentence:

Anokhi, Adonay Elohekha—I am your God.

But *Anokhi* derives from the Egyptian word *Ankho* or *Ankh*, while the Hebrew word for *I* is *Ani*.

In Spain, Rabbi Yehuda Halevi (1075–1141) once asked his contemporary, Rabbi Abraham Ibn Ezra (1089–1167), why the Ten Commandments begin with the letter Alef using the word *Anokhi*—I—based on the Egyptian word *Ankh*, as in "I am your God that took you out of Egypt and slavery" and not—"I am your God that created worlds." After all, he contended, the wonder of creation is much greater than the exodus of Egypt.

Serab el Khadem
Sinai, Proto-Canaanite
1500 BCE

Proto-Canaanite
13th–12th BCE

Ahiram Sarcophagus
Phoenician
1000 BCE

Gezer Calendar
Hebrew
End of 10th century BCE

Mesha Stete
Hebrew Script
Mid 9th century BCE

Kilamu Inscription
Phoenician last third
of 9th century BCE

Siloam Inscription
Hebrew
Late 8th century BCE

Hebrew Seals
7th century BCE

Hebrew Ostraca
Arad
Early 6th century BCE

Elephantine Papyrus
Aramaic
Late 5th century BCE

Leviticus Scroll, Qumran
Paleo-Hebrew
Late 2nd century BCE

Samaritan Manuscript
13th century BCE

Isaiah Scroll I Qumran
Square Hebrew Script
Late 2nd century BCE

A
Classical Greek Script

A
Latin Script

Nabataean Script
1st century BCE

ا
Classical
Arabic Script

To which Rabbi Ibn Ezra replied:

"After all, everyone saw the Exodus from Egypt, but no one saw creation."

Adam, אדם—which starts with an Alef—was the first Man, whom God created on the sixth day. Adam stems from the word *Adama* meaning "earth." At the time of creation, legend has it that Adam's head reached all the way to heaven. Sure enough, Adam looked into the heavens and saw the chaos and the bedlam, and when the angels saw Adam's head poking into their domain, they took a fright, pleading with God:

"God of the Universe! What *'khutspah'* for the first man to meddle in our habitat, he is not even an Angel."

So God rested his hand upon Adam's head and made him much smaller.

Words that begin with Alef are numerous. We have two volumes entitled *The Dictionary of the Yiddish Language* dedicated exclusively to the letter Alef, written by Yudl Mark, a Yiddish scholar.

The Hebrew word *Emet*—אמת—begins with Alef and represents truth.

People say אמן—Amen, which originates with the Hebrew word *Emuna*—אמונה: Belief.

Arabic: *Amina Amuna*—faithful, reliable and trustworthy

Ethiopian: *Amana*—was firm

Syriac: *Amin*—strong, enduring, true, lasting, eternal

Yiddish Proverbs

דער וואָס זאָגט אלף-דער מוז זאָגן בית

Der vos zogt Alef der muz zogn Beyz

He who says Alef, must also say Beyz.

Meaning: He who begins to study

from the beginning must proceed.

דער אמת שטאַרבט קיינמאל נישט
עס לעבט ־ נאָר אַ פּאַסקודנע לעבן

Der emes shtarbt keynmol nisht

Es leybt—nor a paskudne leybn

Truth never dies—but it lives a wretched life.

אַ שווערער בײַטל
מאַכט אַ לײַכט געמיט

A shverer baytl makht a laykht gemit.

A heavy purse makes for a light heart.

אויב איך וועל זײַן ווי ער
ווער וועט זײַן ווי איך

Oyb ikh vel zayn vi er, ver vet zayn vi ikh?

If I am to be like him, who will be like me?

אסימילאַציע

Yiddish—*Asimelatzye*

Assimilation

"Assimilation could be compared to an express train,
at every station it devours a bunch of people."
—CHAIM NAKHMAN BIALIK

ב Bet

ב Yet

ב Bet ב Vet

Numeric Value of 2

Bet represents—בית—*Bayit*

Represents a house or a home in
Ugaric, Phoenician, Aramaic, Syriac

Arabic—Bi'in   Ethiopian—Ba'in

Greek—Beta

God began creating the world with the letter Bet.

The Torah starts with *Breyshit*—בראשית—In the beginning…

Because its numeric value is 2, the mystics emphasize that it represents two worlds: this world and the world to come.

בראשית

Breyshit

In the Beginning

Our creation began before the actual creation, as the Midrash, post-Talmudic literature, states that God created many worlds. He would take one look at each new world He created and then He destroyed all the previous worlds.

God finally undertook to create the world we live in, still, before He created our world, He created:

At the same time, God also created the Holy Temple that sits in waiting for the Messiah's coming and the Magic Cane, with which Moses split the Red Sea. This was no simple cane. On it He carved the Name of God and the names of our biblical patriarchs and matriarchs: Abraham, Isaac and Jacob, Sarah, Rifkah, Rachel, and Leah, the Twelve Tribes, and the first initials of the Ten Plagues.

It is written that when the Messiah finally comes, he will bring with him the Magic Cane of Moses.

בענטשן
Yiddish—*Bentsch'n*
Latin—*Benedicere*
To Bless

One more curiosity connected to the second letter of the Hebrew alphabet is the story of Bethlehem:

בית לחם
Hebrew—*Bet Lekhem*
Bethlehem, lit. House of Bread

The Story of "Bedlam"

The English expression *bedlam*—noise and confusion—has its roots in "Bethlehem." Bedlam was also the name of a London "lunatic" asylum. In the fifteenth century, the Bedlam Asylum was one of the most popular "sightseeing" spots of London. For a modest fee, people could watch the inmates behind bars, much as we view animals in the zoo today. Bethlehem is still in the center of Middle Eastern bedlam.

During Biblical times, people worshiped idols of the sun or the moon, including a pagan Canaanite god named Baal. The Old Testament speaks of the Canaanite Queen Jezebel, wife of King Ahab of Israel.

The only thing that has remained of Baal are the following words both in Hebrew and in Yiddish.

בעל הבית
Hebrew—*Baal Habayit*
Yiddish—*Baleboz; Baleboste*
Master/mistress of the house,
a landlord, a boss.

Yiddish Proverbs

יעדער בעל הבית האָט פֿליי אין דער נאָז
Yeder Baleboz hot fliy in der noz
Every boss has fleas in his nose.
Meaning: The boss can do anything.

הונגער איז אַ בייזער בעל הבית
Hunger iz a beyzer Baleboz
Hunger is a mean master.

גוט צו זײַן אַ בעל הבית אַז ס'איז דאָ מיט װאָס.
Gut tzu zayn a Baleboz az s'iz do mit vos
Good to be the boss if you have the money.

ב Vet

Represents the sound V

Vet is represented in words like:

הבל הבלים

Hevel Havalim

Vanity of Vanities or Chaos

הבדלה

Havdalah

To make a distinction; also an important Jewish religious ceremony performed at the end of the Sabbath, making a distinction between the holy and the profane

	Serab el Khadem Sinai, Proto-Canaanite 1500 BCE
	Proto-Canaanite 13th–12th BCE
	Ahiram Sarcophagus Phoenician 1000 BCE
	Gezer Calendar Hebrew End of 10th century BCE
	Mesha Stete Hebrew Script Mid 9th century BCE
	Kilamu Inscription Phoenician last third of 9th century BCE
	Siloam Inscription Hebrew late 8th century BCE
	Hebrew Seals 7th century BCE
	Hebrew Ostraca Arad early 6th century BCE
	Elephantine Papyrus Aramaic Late 5th century BCE
	Leviticus Scroll, Qumran Paleo-Hebrew Late 2nd century BCE
	Samaritan Manuscript 13th century BCE
	Isaiah Scroll I Qumran Square Hebrew Script Late 2nd century BCE
	Classical Greek Script
	Latin Script
	Nabataean Script 1st century BCE
	Classical Arabic Script

ג Siml

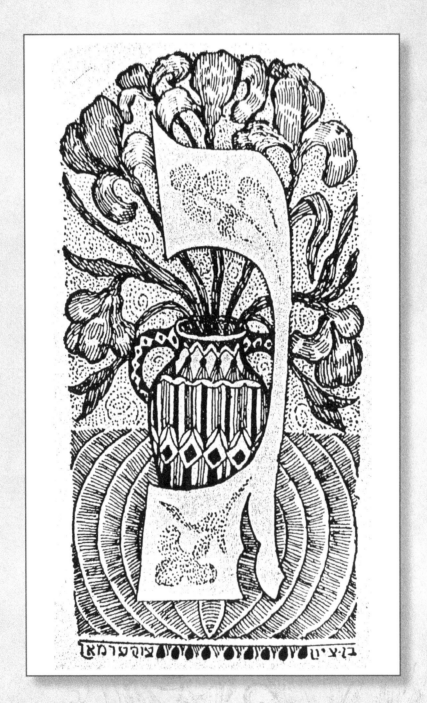

בלצין צופטערמאן

ג Giml

Numeric Value of 3

Represents a Camel

Hebrew—Gamal   Greek—Gamma

saac Luria Ashkenazi, known as the Ari, the central figure of the new Kabbalah in Safed, Palestine of the sixteenth century, was visited by an equally important mystic, Khayim Vital.

Said the Ari to Khayim:

> "I can see all the 22 letters shining on your forehead, except for the letter Giml, which is upside down."

Disturbed by the revelation, Reb Khayim asked the Ari for his interpretation, to which the Ari replied:

> "You are not generous enough with *Gemilat-Khesed*, loving kindness toward your father, in spite of being a good son."

And if one does מצוות (Hebrew—*Mitsvot;* Yiddish—*Mitsves;* English—Good Deeds), the act is recorded by one letter that appears on a man's forehead. The letter begins to glow only when the good deed is repeated for a second time.

גאָט
Yiddish—*Gott*
God

A Fable

Rabbi Zusye, who tried hard to develop the potential of each and every one of his students, would tell them: *When I die and God asks me, in the world to come, why I wasn't Moses, I will tell Him because I was too busy being myself.*

Ironic Yiddish Proverbs About God

גאָט העלף מיר אַרויפֿצוקריכן אויפֿן לײטער
אַראָפּ וועל איך שוין אַליין קענען.

Got helf mir aroyfkrikhn oyfn layter,
arop vel ikh shoyn aleyn kenen.

God help me to go up the ladder,
I can descend myself.

גאָט איז אַן אַלטער קונצנמאַכער

Gott iz an alter kuntznmakher

God is an old magician.

אַז גאָט זאָל וווינען אויף דיֿרערד
וואָלט מען אים אלע פֿענצטער אויסגעהאַקט

Az Gott zol voynen oyf D'rerd
Volt man im ale fenster oysgehakt

If God lived on Earth,
people would break all his windows.

גורל
Hebrew—*Goral* • Yiddish—*Goyrl*
Destiny

We were born into a mysterious universe, into a world of disasters, plagues and evil among men. We should have realized early on that we are hardly in control of our Destiny.

גן עדן און גהינום
Gan Eden and Gehenom
Paradise (The Garden of Eden) and Hell

The Legend of the Divine Keys

On the second day, God created Paradise and Hell and a pair of keys. With these divine keys, one could unlock all the treasures of both worlds. It is written in the Talmud Yerushalmi (Jerusalem Talmud), that when Nebuchadnezzar, the Emperor of Babylonia, conquered Jerusalem, the King of Judah took the keys of the Holy Temple, went up on the roof, and called out to God:

> "Lord of the Universe! Up until now we've kept the keys to your Holy Temple because you believed in us; now that you have stopped loving us, you can have your keys back."

He threw the keys to heaven.

At that very moment, a hand appeared from heaven and took the keys away.

"The Key" (Folklore)

In the town of Progeh, not far from Warsaw in Poland, there lived a wealthy man, a Torah scholar and very charitable philanthropist.

He was known as Reb Fayveleh.

His wife, Rukhl-Leye, was a righteous and a pious woman. Not only was she the matriarch of the family—the *mishpukhe*—but she was the primary provider of the family, enabling Reb Fayveleh to sit day and night in the synagogue and study the Holy Torah. The entire family wealth was due to Rukhl-Leye's diligent toil. She took every hardship easier, knowing that she was doing a great deed—a *Mitzvah*—in making it possible for her husband to sit and study the Holy scriptures.

There came a day, and Reb Fayveleh passed away, and the entire town mourned his passing. It turns out that every pious Jew has a home waiting in *Gan-Eydn*, the Garden of Eden, in the world to come. Every good deed is rewarded with a holy brick, and brick by brick the house is built, the more *mitsves*, good deeds, the more luxurious the estate in the upper world.

If, on the other hand, a Jew doesn't perform any good deeds, their place in the Garden of Eden is overgrown with thistle and thorns.

When Reb Fayveleh ascended to heaven, he was escorted by an Angel to a magnificent home with great big windows. Through the windows Reb Fayveleh could see furniture made out of mahogany wood, giant rooms and mirrors with holy ornaments everywhere.

The Angel led him to the front door of his palace, but Reb Fayveleh found the door locked.

"Where is the key to my heavenly house?" asked Reb Fayveleh.

The Angel answered: "The key is well protected and waiting for its proper owner to arrive."

Reb Fayveleh responded: "I don't understand. Who is the proper owner?"

The Angel answered: "Your wife."

"My wife?" cried out Reb Fayveleh. "With my wife, Rukhl Leye? Why does she have the key? After all, I was the one who studied the scriptures and performed all the good deeds."

Says the Angel: "It's true, you were the one that did all the *mitsves*, the good deeds, you prayed and studied. But who made that possible? Who worried about you every moment of the day? Who took care of your family? Who gave birth and raised the children? Who provided for you? Who gave you the money for all of your *tsdoke* (charity)?"

Reb Fayveleh sat down on the porch of his luxurious dwelling, and he sat, and he sat for years, until his wife, Rukhl Leye, bless her soul, arrived in heaven with the key.

גלאָז
Yiddish—*Gloz*
Glass

What Do You See? (A Legend)

One day, a poor man came to his rabbi complaining: "Rebbe, why are there so many poor people, while others are rich?"

The rabbi said: "Come with me to the window and tell me what you see."

The poor man looked out the window and said: "I see people, I see trees, I see flowers, I see birds, I see children..."

The Rebbe replied: "Come with me to the mirror. Now, tell me what you see."

The man said: "I see my face, I see my nose, I see my eyes, I see my chin..."

Said the Rebbe: "You see good man, both the window and the mirror are made out of glass, but the mirror's back is silvery, so you see only yourself. And the same goes for a rich man, he is a man like you and me, but his pockets are full of silver and gold, so he often sees only himself."

⊤ Dalet

ד Dalet

Numeric Value of 4

Hebrew: Delet—represents door

Symbolizes Security

דאַוונַענעט

Yiddish—Davenen

Praying—From the Latin *Divinus*

Related to Divine and Divinity

The Koretser Rebbe once said: "I love to pray when the sun rises, before the world gets polluted with hatred and wrath."

> דוד המלך
> Hebrew—*Daveed Hamelekh*
> Yiddish—*Dovid Hameylekh*
> King David

The Bible tells us that Israel had three kings: King Saul, King David, and King Solomon.

King Saul was envious of David and feared that he was out to do him harm in order to gain the throne.

King David was the warrior king, constantly battling surrounding enemies. It is said that one day he glanced across his roof and spotted a most beautiful woman named Bat Sheva (Bathsheba), who was married to

Uriyah Hakhitti from the tribe of the Khittites, a warrior tribe constantly engaged in battle with David's Kingdom of Israel.

King David was so enamored with Bat Sheva that he sent her husband, Uriyah, to the front lines to be killed. David then took Bat Sheva for his ninth wife.

King Solomon, David's son, was known for his wisdom and for bringing peace to the region. He had 800 wives and 200 concubines, mostly princesses of nearby kingdoms, that protected him from invasions of warrior kingdoms.

A Chapter from Itzik Manger's
The Book of Paradise

The entire story takes place in Paradise.

We heard the galloping of a steed, who could it be? The rider was so armored that he shimmered in the light of the moon.

The rider jumped off his horse and approached King David's Palace: "Hey David! Get up, let's fight!"

Nobody stirred in the palace except for King David, who came out on the balcony and shouted back: "I know who you are. You are Saul, why don't you let me sleep in peace?"

King Saul laughed, bitter and full of pain.

King David yawned and replied: "Saul! I have no intentions of battling you in Paradise. I came here to relax, to find peace, pleasure and to enjoy the beauty of eternity and its surroundings."

"Coward!" thundered King Saul. "You are afraid of losing the battle this time, I want my crown back!"

To which King David replied: "Be a nice guy and get back on your horse, and be gone, back to the land of Chaos, you are disturbing the sleep of the righteous!"

It is also told of King David that he used to sit on his balcony and play on his harp while the wind gently caressed the strings. The King composed passionate melodies for his biblical Psalms.

דלילה

Delilah

Delilah (lit. of the night)
was Samson's Philistine wife

The Legend of Samson & Delilah

Samson, known as Simshon Hagibor, Samson the Hero or the Great, was the last of the biblical judges. It was believed that his strength emanated from the length of his hair.

There were skirmishes among the people of Israel and the Philistines (not related to the Palestinians of today). Delilah was convinced by her people to betray her husband.

Samson was captured by his enemies, blinded, and placed between two big pillars and ridiculed.

Samson grabbed the two pillars and they fell, killing him and all the enemies that surrounded him.

די דין־תורה מיט גאָט

Di Din Toyre mit Got

The lawsuit brought against God

A Legend About Rabbi Levi Yitzkhak

In the town of Berditchev, where the well-known Rabbi Levi Yitzkhak the Berditchever lived, he once met up with Rabbi Zisl, the Melamed (teacher of young children), who came to him with a grievance against God.

Rabbi Levi Yitzkhak was astounded, thinking that Reb Zisl had probably experienced a tragedy or an injustice.

Rabbi Levi Yitzkhak said: "What is it that bothers you?"

Reb Zisl began his tale of woe:

"I live in terrible poverty, I have a wife and daughter, our only child, who needs to be married, but I cannot afford to pay her dowry or for her wedding. I have come to the conclusion that God is responsible to pay for my daughter's marriage, knowing full well how hard I work studying the Torah, and therefore cannot make a decent living."

Rabbi Levi Yitzkhak, the Berditchiver Hassidic Rabbi (1740–1809), was known for both conversing with and complaining to God in Yiddish on behalf of his people, Israel.

Rabbi Levi Yitzkhak listened carefully to Zisl's complaint and asked him: "Do you have a groom already or is it only a matter of money?"

"For sure!" answered Reb Zisl. "In the old synagogue in town there sits a young man studying the Torah, his name is Yankev Moyshe, and he has agreed to marry my daughter, but I need 300 Rubles for the dowry."

Rabbi Levi Yitzkhak thought for a moment and replied: "According to your complaint, I assume that you are right, but there is a possibility that the One Above does not approve of the match, so I suggest, come back in three days while I get to know the groom. I will have an answer for you then."

Three days later, Rabbi Zisl returned and asked for the verdict.

Rabbi Levi Yitzkhak responded: "I went to see the groom, examined him and came to the conclusion that he is truly a Torah scholar. Therefore, you have won the suit against God and he owes you 300 Rubles."

"If that is the case," shouted Reb Zisl, "I want a written document of the verdict."

"Excellent!" replied Rabbi Levi Yitzkhak. "I will sit down and write the following: *As I have witnessed and listened to Reb Zisl's complaint against God, my verdict is the following: I implore the Jewish Community of Berditchev to supply 300 Rubles to Reb Zisl, the sum owed him by the Almighty for his daughter's wedding expenses and dowry.*"

The Jewish community of Berditchev provided the 300 Rubles and within a week the engagement took place and the wedding occurred the following Sabbath. All of Berditchev came to the wedding that had been arranged by none other than the One Above.

Rabbi Levi Yitzkhak himself performed the wedding ceremony that took place outside. The beadle lowered the glass cup to be stamped on in honor of the destruction of the Temple in Jerusalem, but the glass cup would not shatter and began to sink into the ground.

"Break the glass!" ordered Rabbi Levi Yitzkhak of the groom, but the glass cup sank deeper and deeper into the ground. Shovels were brought in while the Rabbi shouted: "Deeper! Deeper! Dig deeper!"

And suddenly the diggers discovered a rusted tin box filled with gold coins.

Rabbi Levi Yitzkhak said: "Zisl! This money belongs to you. It is the Almighty himself who has paid you many times over because you believed in Him so fervently."

On the spot where the treasure was found, Reb Zisl ordered a synagogue to be built.

	Serab el Khadem Sinai, Proto-Canaanite 1500 BCE
	Proto-Canaanite 13th–12th BCE
	Ahiram Sarcophagus Phoenician 1000 BCE
	Gezer Calendar Hebrew End of 10th century BCE
	Mesha Stete Hebrew Script Mid 9th century BCE
	Kilamu Inscription Phoenician last third of 9th century BCE
	Siloam Inscription Hebrew late 8th century BCE
	Hebrew Seals 7th century BCE
	Hebrew Ostraca Arad early 6th century BCE
	Elephantine Papyrus Aramaic Late 5th century BCE
	Leviticus Scroll, Qumran Paleo-Hebrew Late 2nd century BCE
	Samaritan Manuscript 13th century BCE
	Isaiah Scroll I Qumran Square Hebrew Script Late 2nd century BCE
	Classical Greek Script
	Latin Script
	Nabataean Script 1st century BCE
	Classical Arabic Script

ה Hey

Numeric Value of 5

Represents a little window or fence

ey is a letter of uncertain origin; the mystics believed that the Hey represents a window with bars. In Kabbalah, it symbolizes the idea of love and passion.

Rabi Abahu said in the name of Rabi Yokhanan:

"With the power of two letters, two worlds were created, the lower world with the letter Hey and the upper world with the letter Yud."

And he added:

"With the letter Hey, God created Heaven and Earth, with the letter Yud, He created the world to come."

> הונגער
>
> Yiddish—*Hoonger*
>
> Hunger

Legend of the Wise Rebbe

In one of the little *shtetlekh* there lived a wise Rebbe. One day, several people showed up and told him that their friend Chaim-Yankl had died of hunger.

"What do you mean he died of hunger? After all he could have chopped wood, swept the streets, carried pails of water…"

But the Rebbe was told that the man was once a rich merchant, so it was beyond his dignity to do menial work.

"If that's the case," the Rebbe continued, "He didn't die of hunger, he died of pride, for if one is willing to work they'll never die of hunger."

Traditions

We greet the Jewish New Year by dipping slices of apple into honey as we wish each other a sweet, healthy, and prosperous New Year.

הָאָניק

Yiddish—*Honik*

Honey

הָאָניק־חודש

Yiddish—*Honik Khoydesh*

Honeymoon

At the family table at dinner time, it was the father who was rewarded with the head of a carp fish, since he was the head of the family.

העכט

Yiddish—*Hekht*

Carp

הער

Yiddish—*Hehr*

Listen

The Legend of the Polish Farmer

Many years ago in Poland there was a Jew who decided to settle in Israel and become a farmer. He approached a Polish farmer to teach him the skills of farming and how to work the soil. After the harvest, the Polish farmer lay down on the ground, put his ear to the earth, and began listening.

The Jew asked him: "What do you hear?"

The peasant told him: "I hear the earth singing!"

The Jew placed his ear to the ground and tried to listen but heard nothing. He turned to the farmer and asked: "Why do I hear nothing at all?"

The farmer smiled and replied: "You hear nothing because this is not your soil and not your land!"

When the same Jew arrived in Israel and became a farmer, after the harvest he placed his ear to the to the ground, and he heard the earth singing.

This time it was his earth and his land.

טעאָדאָר הערצל
Theodore Herzl (1860–1904)
The Founder of Zionism

The Diary of Theodor Herzl

Theodor Herzl was the father of Zionism; he was a Viennese journalist and playwright. In Berlin of 1896, while negotiating with the world leaders of Germany, Britain, Russia, and the Ottoman Empire (today's Turkey, who at that time ruled the entire Middle East including Palestine), he wrote a book entitled *Judenstaat—The Jewish State*.

Herzl's Diary went through a fantastic odyssey of its own. While traveling continents, it was auctioned off in London, England, buried by his son during World War II, and finally rediscovered in the Vilna Ghetto in 1946, after the war. It was miraculously rescued, passing through the

Theodor Herzl

ה	
ᛪ	Serab el Khadem Sinai, Proto-Canaanite 1500 BCE
Ɛ	Proto-Canaanite 13th–12th BCE
ᒋ	Ahiram Sarcophagus Phoenician 1000 BCE
	Gezer Calendar Hebrew End of 10th century BCE
ᛦ	Mesha Stete Hebrew Script Mid 9th century BCE
ᛝ	Kilamu Inscription Phoenician last third of 9th century BCE
ᛟ	Siloam Inscription Hebrew late 8th century BCE
ᛢ	Hebrew Seals 7th century BCE
ᛲ	Hebrew Ostraca Arad early 6th century BCE
ᛟ	Elephantine Papyrus Aramaic Late 5th century BCE
ᛩ	Leviticus Scroll, Qumran Paleo-Hebrew Late 2nd century BCE
᛬	Samaritan Manuscript 13th century BCE
ᛢ	Isaiah Scroll I Qumran Square Hebrew Script Late 2nd century BCE
E	Classical Greek Script
E	Latin Script
ᛝ	Nabataean Script 1st century BCE
ᛮ	Classical Arabic Script

Iron Curtain, stealing through borders and barriers, until reaching its final destination at the YIVO, Jewish Scientific Institute in New York. YIVO was founded in Vilna, Lithuania, in 1925, by its founding father, Dr. Max Weinreich (1894–1969), a prolific Yiddish writer and scholar. Among his books are *Hitler's Professors, Bilder: Images of the History of Yiddish Literature,* and the four volumes of his monumental *History of the Yiddish Language.*

Among the YIVO Board of Directors in Vilna were such luminaries as Dr. Albert Einstein and Sigmund Freud.

In the year 1930, Zalmen Reisen, a researcher in residence at the YIVO in Vilna, was on a visit to London, where Theodore Herzl's Diary was being auctioned off by Herzl's son. The diary is a small book of memoirs that covers the period between 1882 and 1887, in which Theodore Herzl writes about his depression, his doubts, and his overall unhappiness with his private life.

Zalmen Reisen paid a deposit for the diary in the hope of successfully procuring the balance that was due. When Reisen returned to Vilna, he was confronted with the reality of the economic conditions of the YIVO, where all the revenues were exhausted.

The financial state of the organization was so challenging that there was not enough money left for stamps, let alone such luxuries as buying rare manuscripts at auction.

In addition, a riot had broken out in Vilna, which took the form of a pogrom, convincing Dr. Max Weinreich to take immediate steps to attempt to bring it under control. As the Chairman of the Association of Journalists and Writers, he organized a delegation of prominent individuals, who together petitioned the Lithuanian government to put an end to the outrageous riots against the Jews.

Instead of intervening, the news of the Jewish delegation's visit was leaked to the hooligans and gang leaders, and they in turn attacked the YIVO delegation itself with clubs and rocks.

The young Dr. Weinreich was wounded. He lost his vision in one eye due to a bad injury.

There were attempts made to restore his vision, but all in vain. He needed to go to Vienna for an expensive operation, which he could not afford.

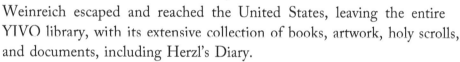

The sum of ten thousand dollars was collected so that Dr. Weinreich could afford to go to Vienna for the operation that would restore his eyesight, but when he went to Vienna instead of having the operation, he gave the money toward the purchase of Herzl's diary, remaining blind in one eye.

Before the Nazis invaded Vilna, Max Weinreich escaped and reached the United States, leaving the entire YIVO library, with its extensive collection of books, artwork, holy scrolls, and documents, including Herzl's Diary.

During the Nazi invasion, the renowned Yiddish poet Avrom Sutzkever was rounded up together with the rest of the Jews of Vilna and confined to the Vilna Ghetto. The Nazis then occupied the YIVO building and ordered several Yiddish poets, historians, and scholars to pack the entire YIVO collection into boxes to be sent to Frankfurt, Germany, where the infamous Rosenberg Shtab would use the collection to build a Museum of the Dead Jewish People.

While the poet Avrum Sutskever was complying with the Nazi order, he came across Herzl's Diary, which he hid in his coat pocket. The diary and other scholarly works that had been smuggled out of the YIVO building were buried underground in the ghetto.

The Yiddish scholar Leyzer Ran returned to Vilna after the war, where he uncovered the buried books, among them Herzl's Diary.

Coming to America in 1946, he was greeted by Dr. Weinreich, now the Director of the YIVO in New York. Leyzer Ran pulled Herzl's Diary out if his vest pocket and presented it to Dr. Weinreich.

Herzl's Diary is now exhibited permanently at the YIVO, which is part of the Center for Jewish History in New York.

ו Vav

Numeric Value of 6

Hebrew—Vav   Yiddish—Vov

n the ancient form of Hebrew, Vav has the meaning of hook, peg, symbol of unity, accord, compassion, and life. It also represents the Tree of Life because of its gentle character.

The Vav is a liaison between extreme powers, mediating between the thirty-two mystical paths of wisdom and the two extremes of the twenty-two letters of the Alef-Bet.

The Torah begins with the letter Beyz—*Breyshit* (In the Beginning)—and ends with the letter Lamed—*Yisroel*.

It is said in the Zohar, the Book of Splendor, that the entire Torah relies on the letter Vav, alluding to the six-thousandth year, the year of redemption.

The Zohar tells the story of Rabi Yosi who was once wandering through a dark cave, where he came across a mysterious book hidden in the crevice of a rock. As soon as he opened the book, he realized that the letters in the book were of a mysterious nature, and before he knew it, a fiery storm erupted and snatched the book from his hands.

When this story was told to Rabi Shimon, he replied: "Rabi Yosi must have come across the mysteries of the Alef-Bet and the numerical value that predicted the end of days and the coming of the Messiah."

> **ווילנע**
> Vilna
> Vilnius, Lithuania

The city of Vilnius in Lithuania was known for their great Jewish scholars.

The City of Vilna, a Fable

One day a Jew ventured out to the city of Vilna; when he came back to his shtetl, he didn't have adequate words to describe what he saw in the big city. And when he was asked by the shtetl-Jews: "So tell us, what have you seen in the city of Vilna?" he replied: "The Vilna Jews are extraordinary people."

So the small-town folk couldn't understand what he meant by extraordinary…

To which the man replied:

I have seen a Jew who swayed back and forth over the Talmud, day and night.

I have seen a Jew that pursued business day and night.

I have seen a Jew running after women day and night.

I have seen a Jew that ran away from women day and night.

I have seen a Jew who ran around with a red flag shouting, 'Revolution,' day and night.

I have seen a Jew who ran around shouting, 'Down with the Revolution,' day and night.

So the shtetl-Jews said to him: "Why are you so amazed? After all, Vilna is a big city. All kinds of Jews live in Vilna."

To which the traveler replied victoriously: "What don't you people understand? I am talking about one and the same Jew!"

The Legend of the Weeping Preacher

Just as there is an assortment of Cantors, there are also different preachers. There are preachers who are master orators, while there are others who speak and it sounds like a melody, while there are still others who excel at crying and weeping.

As it happens, in one shtetl there was a preacher, who was a master at crying. During his sermons, he was so morbid that the walls would weep bitter tears, while he himself used to weep and the entire congregation cried together with him.

Once, he delivered a sermon that about how good it is to be good and pious, and how bad it is to be bad and evil.

To illustrate, he told them the following story:

"Once there was a tailor, healthy and strong, handsome as they come. He had a wife and seven children and worked very hard to eek out a living.

"But one day his luck ran out. He began to smoke on the Sabbath and even began to eat non-kosher food. One day he pricked his finger with his needle while sewing, the blood began to flow, until his right hand had to be amputated."

As soon as the preacher finished the story, all the women began to cry. But the preacher did not stop; he kept spinning his tale:

"A week went by and the tailor's left hand had to be amputated."

The entire synagogue was in tears, including the preacher, but he continued with his tale of woe.

"Still the man didn't conform and didn't mend his ways. He lost all his money, his livelihood, until the town had to support him. A week went by and his right foot had to be amputated."

۹	Serab el Khadem Sinai, Proto-Canaanite 1500 BCE
	Proto-Canaanite 13th–12th BCE
𐤅	Ahiram Sarcophagus Phoenician 1000 BCE
Y	Gezer Calendar Hebrew End of 10th century BCE
Y	Mesha Stete Hebrew Script Mid 9th century BCE
۴	Kilamu Inscription Phoenician last third of 9th century BCE
۴	Siloam Inscription Hebrew late 8th century BCE
۴	Hebrew Seals 7th century BCE
۴	Hebrew Ostraca Arad early 6th century BCE
)	Elephantine Papyrus Aramaic Late 5th century BCE
ﻚ	Leviticus Scroll, Qumran Paleo-Hebrew Late 2nd century BCE
ﺯ	Samaritan Manuscript 13th century BCE
۱	Isaiah Scroll I Qumran Square Hebrew Script Late 2nd century BCE
	Classical Greek Script
F	Latin Script
٩	Nabataean Script 1st century BCE
و	Classical Arabic Script

The entire congregation was weeping hysterically and the more the people cried, the longer the preacher preached.

"So you think the poor man changed? Nothing doing, until he lost his left foot and then one of his eyes and one of his ears, and he remained a cripple for life, but he never mended his ways.

"So cry, my friends, cry your hearts out as you hear the further misfortunes that befell this poor man. And if you think you've heard it all, you haven't heard anything yet."

The outcry of the people was heard outside:

"What could be even worse than that?!"

And so the preacher went on: "Can you imagine, a man without legs, without hands, without his eyes and ears, what could have been worse than that? It was the period when the Czar's army would kidnap every available man to serve, and one day they came upon the poor tailor. They captured him, enlisting him in the Czar's army where they turned him into a soldier."

Now the entire synagogue was weeping, flooding the temple with their tears, but can you imagine the greatest tragedy was yet to come, when the preacher drowned because he couldn't swim.

> ווערעמלעך
> Yiddish—*Veremlakh*
> Worms

Praise the Lord, a Story

"Take a good look, my child, how the One Above has set up everything," said the father to his child.

"The birds lay eggs in their nests, and when they chicks pick at their shells, out come little birds. That's when the father bird and the mother bird begin to feed their young little birds worms, and they thank and praise the Lord for his exceptional goodness."

The child turns to the father and asks: "Father dear, do the little worms also thank and praise the Lord when the little birdies eat them up?"

ז Zayin

ז Zayin

Numeric Value of 7

Represents the words "weapon" and "ornament"

Hebrew word for weapon is—כְּלִי זַיִן—*Kley-Zayin*

Corresponds to numerous ancient languages, among them:

Aramaic—Zana

Syriac—Zanni

Ethiopian—Zeynat

Meaning: Pollution

The primary characteristics of ז is the sword, the hammer, and the bow, signifying symbols of power.

Legend has it that the Zayin came before God and insisted that He create the world with him, after all, he represents the numeric value of seven, through him, the day of Sabbath is observed.

To which God replied:

"I will not create the world with you, for you carry within you the sword and the spear and the lust for war."

זאָג

Yiddish—*Zog*

To Say

A Holocaust Song

זאָג נישט קיין מאָל

DON'T EVER SAY (The Partisan Song)
Written by Hirsh Glick

Never, never say there is no other way

When leaden skies may now conceal the light of day

The hour that we long for will one day appear

Beneath our feet the earth will tremble

WE ARE HERE

This song is written with our blood and not with lead

It's not a song that summer-birds sing overhead

A people fighting among crumbling barricades

We sing this song of ours with pistols and grenades

זײַן
Yiddish—*Zayn*
To Be

Yiddish Shakespeare

> *Tsu zayn oder nisht tsu Zayn*
> To be or not to be
>
> *Do ligt der hunt bagrobn*
> That's where the dog is buried.
> Meaning: That is the question.

Yiddish—*Zol Zayn*

LET'S ASSUME/LET'S SAY/LET IT BE

Song by I. Papiernikov

Let's assume I build all my castles in the air
Let's say that my God does not entirely exist
My dream is much brighter
My dream is much better
In my dream my heaven
Is bluer than blue

Let's say that I'll never reach my goal
Let's say that my ship will never reach the shore
It isn't about having reached
It's about walking on the sunny side of the road

זון

Yiddish—*Zun*

Son

דער זון פֿון מלאך המות

Yiddish—*Der zun fun Malekh Hamoves*

The Son of the Angel of Death

The Son of the Angel of Death, a Legend

Once the Angel of Death descended to earth and married a Jewish woman, a real witch. He was married to her for many years until she gave birth to their son.

When the son turned fifteen, his father, the Angel of Death, had had enough. Bored with his wife, he decided he would rather be in Hell than live with his wife, the witch.

Serab el Khadem Sinai, Proto-Canaanite 1500 BCE
Proto-Canaanite 13th–12th BCE
Ahiram Sarcophagus Phoenician 1000 BCE
Gezer Calendar Hebrew End of 10th century BCE
Mesha Stete Hebrew Script Mid 9th century BCE
Kilamu Inscription Phoenician last third of 9th century BCE
Siloam Inscription Hebrew late 8th century BCE
Hebrew Seals 7th century BCE
Hebrew Ostraca Arad early 6th century BCE
Elephantine Papyrus Aramaic Late 5th century BCE
Leviticus Scroll, Qumran Paleo-Hebrew Late 2nd century BCE
Samaritan Manuscript 13th century BCE
Isaiah Scroll I Qumran Square Hebrew Script Late 2nd century BCE
Classical Greek Script
Latin Script
Nabataean Script 1st century BCE
Classical Arabic Script

But he loved his son, after all he was his father, so before he departed he said to his son:

"My son! I want you to grow up and be a doctor. When you see a patient who is very ill, and you see me at the head of his bed, you will know that this patient will not survive. If I do not appear at the head of the patient, he will recuperate and get well."

When the son grew up, he became a doctor, and a very well-known physician at that. As time passed, the king of the land became very ill and no doctor could find a solution, until the Son of the Angel of Death was contacted and forewarned with these words: "If you don't heal the king, your life will be at stake."

And so the doctor, who was the Son of the Angel of Death, began examining the king. He took the king's pulse—it was barely beating. He looked up, and there at the head of the king's bed stood his father, the Angel of Death, saying: "The King must die!"

When his son, the doctor, heard what his father had to say, he pleaded with him: "Father! Please go away!"

But the father refused, until the son turned to him with this warning: "Father! If you don't leave right now, I will be forced to call my mother!"

The minute the Angel of Death, his father, heard the warning, he immediately disappeared, and the king got well.

Yiddish Proverb

זאָאָלאָגישער גאָרטן

Yiddish—*Zoologisher Gortn*

The Zoological Garden

The Zoological Garden is a place where wild animals are protected from people.

ח Khet

Numeric Value of 8

Hebrew—Khet   Yiddish—Khes

Represents a Fence

het stems from the Assyrian—old Hebrew, the letter resembles a gate; it is also a symbol of violence. The word חי—*Khay*—represents life, while *Khaye* represents a living creature, animal, and violence. Yiddish—*Vilde Khaye* means wild animal.

> חטא
> Hebrew—*Khet*
> Yiddish—*Khes*
> Represents sin

Arabic—*Hatiya*—To make a mistake
Ugaric—*Hatu* represents missing the goal, to sin, to incur guilt

Khet appears in words like:

> חכם
> Hebrew—*Khakham*
> Yiddish—*Khokhem*
> A wise man

The Legend of Eve's Creation

And God had seen how lonely Adam was, He created for him a second wife. And God said:

From what part of Adam's body should I create Eve?

I shall not create her from the head, she should not be proud.

I should not create her from the eyes, she should not be too curious; or from the ear, she should not be too inquisitive; or from the heart, she should not be envious; or from the foot, she should not be fickle; or from the mouth, she should not be a gossip.

I shall create her from Adam's Rib, she should be modest and know humility.

And in spite of all that:

Sarah, our matriarch, was curious—she eavesdropped on God's angels.

Rachel, Jacob's second wife, was envious of her sister, Lea, for marrying Jacob, her beloved, first.

Dina, Jacob's daughter, was fickle and a flirt.

Miriam, the sister of Moses and Aaron, gossiped too much and was punished by being sent off to a leper colony.

*The remorse of the letter Khet touched the heart of King Solomon, who intervened in its behalf with the Celestial Court of Justice, and as a sign of pardon, the letter Khet was also granted the eight days of Khanuka—*הכונח.

Legend About Sin: The Flood

The story is told about the town of Khelm in Poland, where out of the blue the heavens opened and what came down was a flood, reminiscent of Noah's deluge. It nearly drowned everything in sight. So the Khelemites took off to the Rebbe's house with a plea:

"Rebbe Leybn (long life to you, rebbe), do something or we will all be wiped out, and not a sign will remain of us."

So the Rebbe ordered them to say special prayers and implore the One Above to stop this flood.

But to no avail; it became even more severe, as if God's wrath poured out of heaven, consuming the poor town of Khelm.

Finally the Rebbe was struck with an idea. "Someone must be carrying on a sinful and illicit affair in the shtetl, so I command you to go and find the culprits who are committing this abominable sin, only then will God's wrath be soothed."

So the Khelemites set out to find the culprits—they searched and they ransacked every home, every corner of town, until they came across a young Yeshivah (Hebrew Academy) student who was having an illicit affair with a married woman.

In a state of rage, they began cursing and throwing rocks at the sinful couple with the idea of stoning them to death.

When the Rebbe heard what they were doing, he came running with his fists in the air, out of breath shouting at the stone-throwing crowd: "*Gevald Yidn* (Help us, Jews), what are you doing? You have as much brains in your head as a church has *Mezuzas* (Holy inscription on a door jamb)! Idiots! Fools! God forbid you could kill the couple! What if next year we might have a drought here in Khelm? We'll need their services!"

> ## חלום
> Hebrew—*Khalom*
> Yiddish—*Kholem*
> Dream

Affluent ancient Egyptians used to pay others to dream for them.

———◁•▷———

> ## חזיר
> Hebrew—*Khazir*
> Yiddish—*Khazer*
> A Pig, swine, a non kosher animal, forbidden
> in the dietary Jewish and Muslim laws.

The Legend of the Pig Plague

A fascinating story is told of a plague that accosted the pigs in Eastern Europe during the Middle Ages.

When a plague struck the pigs of a shtetl, a little town in Eastern Europe where Jews lived among Gentiles, the Jews would fast.

They fasted because of the superstition that the Angel of Death, when collecting his victims, might skip a Jewish home and instead take a pig, whose beating human heart might confuse him. (The Jews somehow knew instinctively that the pigs had a heart similar to humans. For several decades now, pigs' hearts, valves, and insulin are used on people all over the world while waiting for transplants and medication.)

Chanukah

Chanukah is a relatively young holiday that immortalizes the victories of the Khashmonoyim, during the Babylonian exile (586–538 BCE), when legend has it, one day's worth of oil for the Holy Temple lasted eight days.

Jews no longer had their own kingdom in Israel; they lived under foreign rule. From 539 to 333 BCE, the Persian Empire reigned from India to Ethiopia. For two hundred years, Jews lived under Persian world domination. From Syria to the north of Israel to Egypt in the South, all were under the rule of Persia.

Jews lived in the small and weak land of Judea. Persia gave them full autonomy and didn't mix into their affairs. The Persian governor was in charge of order and collected taxes.

Representing the Judeans was the High Priest Kohen Hagadol. The Judean High Priest became a political leader in the Kingdom of Judea.

This lasted until the fourth century CE when Alexander the Great, the Macedonian, conquered Persia.

The Greeks ruled the world at that time, and Judea became a province of Alexander's world domination during the Hellenic Period (507–323 BCE).

The Greeks also called themselves Helenese. The people under Greek rule were forced to adopt Greek language and culture.

When Alexander the Great passed away and his empire collapsed, both the Syrians and the Egyptians began fighting each other, and the Jews were caught in the middle.

The holiday of Chanukah signifies the rededication of the Second Temple in Jerusalem, at the time of the Maccabean Revolt against the Selucide Empire and the kingdom of Antiyokhus Epiphanus.

It was Judah Hamakabi, the Maccabean, and his followers who liberated the Second Temple in Jerusalem in the year 166 BCE and cleansed it of all its pagan rituals.

Legend has it that they found one jar of pure olive oil with the seal of the *Kohen Gadol,* the High Priest. The jar had only enough oil to burn for one day, but a miracle occurred, and it burned for eight days.

חדר

Hebrew—*Kheder*

Yiddish—*Kheyder*

A room/a religious school for young boys

A Tradition

When a little Jewish boy reaches the age of three, his father would cover him in a prayer shawl and lead him to Kheyder. He covered him in order for his little eyes not to see the impure world.

In Kheyder, the rabbi would write the Alef-Bet on a little writing board, sprinkle them with honey and have the child lick it up, saying: "You see my child how sweet the Jewish Alef-Bet is?"

חורבן
Hebrew—*Khurban*
Yiddish—*Khurb'n*
The Destruction—The Holocaust

Shoah
Hebrew for Holocaust

Holocaust comes from the Greek referring to a sacrificial offering that is wholly consumed by fire; this expression is not rooted in Jewish history nor tradition.

Khurbn—rooted in Jewish history for thousands of years—reminds us of the destruction of ancient Jerusalem, of lost Jewish life, our people, and our cultural heritage.

During all of our exiles, we lived among strangers, tiny specs on the maps of the Middle East and Asia, Poland, Russia, Ukraine, Lithuania, Czechoslovakia, the Carpathian Mountains, Romania, and Bessarabia, among so many others.

A Jewish world where poor little Jewish towns were awash with a rich Jewish landscape and awash in poverty—all lost in the many Holocausts since the destruction of the Holy Temple, the Inquisitions, the Diaspora, and the Shoah.

Π	
𐤄	Serab el Khadem Sinai, Proto-Canaanite 1500 BCE
𐤄	Proto-Canaanite 13th–12th BCE
𐤄	Ahiram Sarcophagus Phoenician 1000 BCE
𐤄	Gezer Calendar Hebrew End of 10th century BCE
𐤄	Mesha Stete Hebrew Script Mid 9th century BCE
𐤄	Kilamu Inscription Phoenician last third of 9th century BCE
𐤄	Siloam Inscription Hebrew late 8th century BCE
𐤄	Hebrew Seals 7th century BCE
𐤄	Hebrew Ostraca Arad early 6th century BCE
𐤄	Elephantine Papyrus Aramaic Late 5th century BCE
𐤄	Leviticus Scroll, Qumran Paleo-Hebrew Late 2nd century BCE
𐤄	Samaritan Manuscript 13th century BCE
ה	Isaiah Scroll I Qumran Square Hebrew Script Late 2nd century BCE
Η	Classical Greek Script
H	Latin Script
ح	Nabataean Script 1st century BCE
ح	Classical Arabic Script

A Story from Peter Malkin

This is the story that Israeli secret agent Peter Malkin tells:

"It was the day when we caught Adolf Eichmann in Argentina, the plane was waiting for us while we carried the murderer onto the plane in order to take him back with us to Israel, where he would stand trial.

"I held his hand in mine and didn't stop thinking, *How could it be, six million Jews waiting at the trains to be deported?* I couldn't imagine it, so I turned to him and said, 'I have seen that you have a nice-looking little boy back where we got you. He reminds me of another child who could have been his little brother, my sister's little boy; with one exception—my sister's little boy is dead.'"

Eichman bit his lip and replied: "Is it my fault that your sister's little boy was Jewish?"

ט Tet

ט Tet

Numeric Value of 9

Hebrew—Tet   Yiddish—Tes

Tet represents clay, dust and earth

Good and Evil, Life and Death

A symbol of Poverty

The letter Tet/Tes occurs in many Semitic languages. It also symbolizes a snake, both because of its elasticity and the state of its curves. Clay and dust are the elements with which the world was created. The letter first appears in the Bible in the word טוב—*Tov*—good.

The Legend of the Magic City

Once there was a magic city over which the Angel of Death had no power, and no one ever died there unless they ventured out of the city gates.

The curious nature of the city began when God's sacred Name appeared engraved in the clouds, hovering and circling over the world. As the world was being created, the letters lined up, one by one, and waited their turn, as they were the instruments of creation.

When God came to the letter Yud, He stopped all of creation, causing the unsuspecting Tet/Tes, that came before Yud, to slip and remain dangling over a certain spot in creation, causing everlasting life.

Legend from the Midrash (the Oral Tradition)

Once there was a papa bird, and he had three little baby birds. His nest was on a very tall tree next to the seashore. One day a horrible storm was brewing, and the papa bird said to his little baby birds: "If we don't fly to the other side of the sea, we will be lost."

But the young birds couldn't fly, so papa bird grabbed the first of his offspring and began the journey across the sea. In the middle of the sea, the papa bird said to his first little bird: "My child, look at the great difficulties I suffer because of you, I endanger my own life to save yours. When I will get old and weak, will you be as good to me as I am to you now?"

The first little bird answered: "My dear father, just bring me to the other side of the sea, and I will be good to you when you're old and weak."

As soon as the papa bird heard this answer, he threw the young bird into the sea saying: "That's what you do with a liar!"

Back went the papa bird to pick up his second offspring. He flew with him over the sea, and in the midst of the journey, he confronted him with the same question: "Will you do for me what I am doing for you when I get old and weak?"

The second bird answered: "I'll do everything for you that you are doing for me, as long as you get me to the other side of the stormy sea."

As soon as the papa bird heard this reply, he threw the baby bird into the water shouting after him: "You big liar!"

In this political cartoon, the eagle represents the American Jewish community financially supporting the Jewish settlements in British-mandated Palestine.

Courtesy of YIVO Institute for Jewish Research

The papa bird flew back to his nest and picked up his last little bird. Once they were in the middle of the journey, the papa bird asked his offspring the same question: "Do you see how I endanger my life to save you? Will you do the same for me when I will get old and weak?"

The last little bird answered: "My dear father, I see how hard it is for you to save and protect me. It will be my obligation to return this favor to you if at all possible. All I can tell you is this, if I will ever have little birds, I will certainly do for them what you are doing for me."

The papa bird was satisfied with his answer and saved him.

טרייף
Treyf
Non Kosher

Milk and meat products cannot be mixed, as it is said: **You cannot boil meat in mother's milk.**

———◁•▷———

טויט-שרעק
Toyt-Shrek
Extreme Fright

A Legend About Reb Dovidl

Reb Dovidl, the Tchernobiler Rabbi (The Rabbi of Chernobyl), was known as a healer. Not only did he distribute blessings, but also amulets and all kinds of mixtures of ointments and herbal remedies.

He knew the power of herbs by immersing himself in the *Sefer Harefuot—The Ancient Book of Remedies.*

One day he was visited by a man who complained that his feet were made out of glass and that he was afraid to sit down for fear of breaking them. The man kept on standing and walking, but never sitting down or lying down. As many times as the man had been told that his legs are not made out of glass, he would not change his mind.

People thought he was possessed by a Dybbuk, a wandering, dead soul.

"I cannot sit down," he cried, "I'm afraid my glass feet will break and I will become a cripple."

After consulting with his Shames, his synagogue caretaker, the rabbi cried out: "Sit! I implore you to sit!"

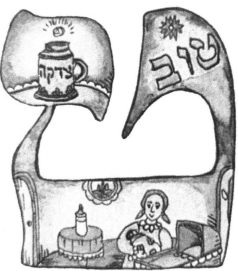

The man was petrified, but if the rabbi gives you an order, you must do as the rabbi tells you.

The man sat down and suddenly he heard a crash of breaking glass, the glass in his feet broke, and the man immediately felt the flesh and bones in his feet.

To which Reb Dovidl replied: "You see, the glass broke and your feet remained intact."

The man was ecstatic and went home full of joy.

Reb Dovidl's Hassidim, his followers, asked him: "Rabbi, how did you accomplish this miracle?"

The rabbi responded: "My dear Hassidim, you see, before I told the man to sit down, I instructed my Shames in the kitchen to break a couple of plates and cups, so that this sick man should think that it came from his legs."

Note: This story was told by Reb Duvidl from the city of Tchernoble in the Ukraine. This story also appears in Textbooks of Psychology in America, *according to Dr. Arnie Richards, a renowned psychologist.*

ט

Serab el Khadem
Sinai, Proto-Canaanite
1500 BCE

Proto-Canaanite
13th–12th BCE

Ahiram Sarcophagus
Phoenician
1000 BCE

Gezer Calendar
Hebrew
End of 10th century BCE

Mesha Stete
Hebrew Script
Mid 9th century BCE

Kilamu Inscription
Phoenician last third
of 9th century BCE

Siloam Inscription
Hebrew
late 8th century BCE

Hebrew Seals
7th century BCE

Hebrew Ostraca
Arad
early 6th century BCE

Elephantine Papyrus
Aramaic
Late 5th century BCE

Leviticus Scroll, Qumran
Paleo-Hebrew
Late 2nd century BCE

Samaritan Manuscript
13th century BCE

Isaiah Scroll I Qumran
Square Hebrew Script
Late 2nd century BCE

Classical Greek Script

Latin Script

Nabataean Script
1st century BCE

Classical
Arabic Script

טײ
Yiddish—*Tey*
Tea

די נײַעסטע סאָרטן כינעזישע טײ
(the newest sorts of Chinese tea)

LIBER-TEA

EQUALI-TEA

FRATERNI-TEA

׳ **Yud**

Numeric Value of 10

Hebrew—Yod   Yiddish—Yud

Smallest letter in the Alef-Bet

Related to Hebrew—(Hebrew word)—*Yad*—Hand

English—*Iota*, the smallest object

According to legend, all the letters of the Hebrew alphabet are rooted in the letter Yud. Although the smallest of all the letters, it is a symbol of strength, possession, determination, eternity, and divine power. The most mysterious of all the words in the Bible is the name of God, which begins with the letter Yud.

The name of God consists of the holy letters יהוה—referred to as Yahveh/Yehavah/Jehovah.

In spite of its diminutive size, it is said that the world to come was created by virtue of the letter Yud, to accommodate the small number of *Tsadikim*, righteous men.

׳׳
Yi sound

ייד
Yiddish—*Yid*
Jew

The old age question is asked:
Who is a Jew?
The answer is:
One who will have Jewish grandchildren.

———◁•▷———

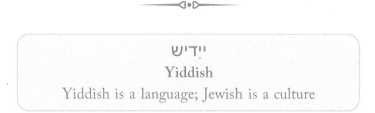

יִידִישׁ

Yiddish

Yiddish is a language; Jewish is a culture

Yiddish is the language of Ashkenazi Jews that is over 1,000 years old.

Originating in Central and Eastern Europe, Yiddish is fused with Biblical Hebrew, Jewish Aramaic, Latin, Greek, Medieval German, plus Slavic languages, namely our 2,000-year-old journey under duress through European exile. It is a controversial language, carrying ancient ideas, spirituality, humor, melodies, and dialects.

Yiddish is a distinct Jewish language and not an adopted tongue of a host country. It bonded itself into the historic fibers of the Jewish people, into their traditions, folk memory, and ancient wisdom.

A *Yiddishe Neshome* is a Jewish soul that longs to return to its source.

Yiddish planted her roots on many a foreign soil, blossoming under all skies, and yet a stranger at all times.

Yiddish words and expressions have become an integral part of modern mainstream language and culture: A *Gantse Megilleh,* it's a long, involved story.

Khutspah derives from the Hebrew meaning the brazen, the nerve, the gall and arrogance.

Yiddish curses are especially biting:

> *Zolst vaksn vi a tsibele mitn kop in dr'erd.*
> You should grow like an onion with your head in the ground.

> *Dayne tseyn zoln zikh tsebeyzern un aropshlingen dem kop.*
> May your teeth get angry at you and chew off your head.

Zolst farlirn ale dayne tseyn, bloyz eyner zol blaybn oyf tsonveytik.
You should lose all of your teeth, except one, in which you should
  have a terrible toothache.

Der Malekh-Hamoves zol zikh in dir farlibn.
May the Angel of Death fall in love with you.

M'gilgl zol er vern in a heng-laykhter,
  Bay tog zol er hengen un bay nakht zol er brenen.
May he die and be reincarnated as a magnificent chandelier.
  He should hang all day and burn all night.

Zol im dunern in boykh un blitsn in di hoyzn.
  May he experience thunder in his belly and lightning in his pants.

Language is the soul of the people. God created the world using words. Language is a means of communication.

Jewish culture has maintained its continuity for over 5,000 years in the face of persecutions, expulsions, massacres, from medieval times and into the twenty-first century.

One of our Yiddish bards, Jacob Glatstein, wrote in one of his poems the following lines:

"Without Jews, there will be no Jewish God."

An Excerpt of Isaac Bashevis-Singer's Speech

(Delivered in Stockholm, Sweden, when he received the 1978 Nobel Prize for Literature)

"The high honor bestowed upon me by the Swedish Academy is also a recognition of the Yiddish language, a language of exile, without a land, without frontiers, not supported by any government. A language which possesses no words for weapons, ammunition, military exercises and war tactics.

"One can find in the Yiddish tongue and in the Yiddish style expressions of pious joy, lust for life, longing for the Messiah, patience and a deep appreciation of human individuality.

"There is quiet humor in Yiddish and a gratitude for every day of life, every crumb of success, each encounter of love.

"The Yiddish mentality is not haughty, it does not take victory for granted, it does not demand and command, but it muddles through, sneaks by, smuggles itself amid the powers of destruction, knowing somewhere that God's plan for creation is still at the very beginning.

"Yiddish has not yet said its last word, it contains treasures that have yet to be revealed to the eyes of the world. It is the tongue of martyrs and

Isaac Bashevis-Singer, winner of the 1978 Nobel Prize for Literature.

saints, of dreamers and mystics, rich in humor and memories that mankind may never forget.

"In a figurative way, Yiddish is the wise and humble language of us all, the idiom of a frightened and hopeful humanity."

YIDDISH

by Moyshe Nadir

Moyshe Nadir

What should our national Jewish language be?

In my mind it should be Loshn Koydesh, the Sacred Tongue, provided it is spoken in Yiddish.

Yiddish is the most desirable language in the world, it possesses the charm, freshness and vitality of a language that lives on the periphery.

It is more sacred than the sacred tongue, it is a language anointed with blood, sanctified with tears, it has not the false prettiness or powdered face, it flows smoothly...

All you have to do is open your mouth and it flows...

What could be simpler than that?

ר	
ے	Serab el Khadem Sinai, Proto-Canaanite 1500 BCE
ᒥ	Proto-Canaanite 13th–12th BCE
ך	Ahiram Sarcophagus Phoenician 1000 BCE
ㄹ	Gezer Calendar Hebrew End of 10th century BCE
ユ	Mesha Stete Hebrew Script Mid 9th century BCE
ユ	Kilamu Inscription Phoenician last third of 9th century BCE
ユ	Siloam Inscription Hebrew late 8th century BCE
ᘔ	Hebrew Seals 7th century BCE
ᐈ	Hebrew Ostraca Arad early 6th century BCE
ᐃ	Elephantine Papyrus Aramaic Late 5th century BCE
ᐟ	Leviticus Scroll, Qumran Paleo-Hebrew Late 2nd century BCE
m	Samaritan Manuscript 13th century BCE
ᒉ	Isaiah Scroll I Qumran Square Hebrew Script Late 2nd century BCE
I	Classical Greek Script
I	Latin Script
ر	Nabataean Script 1st century BCE
ﺯ	Classical Arabic Script

יצר הרע
Yiddish—*Yetser Hore* • Hebrew—*Yetzer Hara*
Evil inclination

Yetser Hore consists of two words, *Yetser/Yetsire*, representing Creation, and Ha Ra for Evil Inclination, the seducer, the evil Angel that tempts you to sin and to do evil deeds. God also created the:

יצר טוב
Yetser Tov
The good inclination, the will to do good.

⊲•⊳

יד ושם
Yad Vashem
Yad is a place; *Shem* is a name.

Yad Vashem: "a place and a name," for those who were not given the dignity of a Jewish burial—or any burial at all—in millions of cases.

Yad Vashem is a museum in Jerusalem commemorating the victims of the Holocaust.

ף כ Kaf

כ Kaf כ Khaf

Numeric Value of 20

Hebrew—Kaf

Hebrew—Khaf

Yiddish—Kof

Yiddish—Khof

ך Khaf Sofit

Final Khaf—at the end of a word

af represents the hollow of your palm and is the symbol of purity and virtue.

> כעלם
> *Khelm*
> The Town of Fools

The Legend of the Town of Fools

Prewar Khelm was a real Jewish town in Poland, but in our folklore, we have classified Khelm as the town of *Khelemer Naronim,* the "Foolish Folks of Khelm."

They were the objects of ridicule, serving as the basis for many popular stories and fables. In reality, Khelm was a town like all other towns, breeding wise men and scholars, educators, and plain folk.

We were not the only ones to invent a town of fools; there were the *Wise Men of Gotham*, in twelfth-century Nottinghamshire, an allusion to an incident where they supposedly feigned idiocy to avoid a royal visit.

The Syrians regarded Homs as their Khelm of dullards; the Persians tell stories of Geelan as the town of simpletons, the Greeks had Boeotia, a city of incredibly witless folk.

"Khakme Khelm" Illustration by F. Halperin (Warsaw, 1926)

The French scoffed at the countrymen of Saint Maixent; the Scotts derided the men of Cupar in Fife; the Germans poked fun at the residents of Swabia and Schildburg; the Italians laughed at the inhabitants of Zago, who fertilized the steeple of their church to make it grow taller; even the good-natured Dutch ascribed stupidity to the Belgians.

Khelm was a city in Poland, and although it still exists geographically, it is no longer a Jewish city. The Holocaust wiped Khelm off the map—almost all the Jews of Khelm perished in Auschwitz and Majdanek Death Camps. But the memory of the Khelm Jews, both the wise and the foolish ones, will remain with us forever.

And if you think Khelm was inhabited by fools, listen to this true story about an Alderman at a meeting of the City Council of New York in the 1940s.

One New York City official said: "To beautify Central Park I recommend we import Gondolas from Venice, Italy and let them swim around our beautiful lake.

Another city councilman intervened: "Take pity on New York taxpayers, they are over burdened as it is paying very high taxes."

A third councilman interrupted: "I suggest we import only two gondolas from Venice, a male and a female, and when they mate we will have plenty of gondolas to go around." (Gondolas are small boats.)

The Khelemite Oven, a Legend

On a simple old Wednesday, the Jews of Khelm decided to buy an oven for the Synagogue. The problem was where to put the oven, what the oven should be made of, and what it would cost.

One day between the afternoon and evening prayers, the townspeople assembled to discuss the oven.

One of them said: "The oven should be made out of iron."

Another said: "I insist it should be made out of tile."

But they all decided that iron and tile were a bit too expensive.

Suddenly Berl jumped up and said: "Gentlemen! I will help you. I am

blessed with lots of animals on my farm, I have plenty of flour and butter, more than I need, more than I can sell, so I suggest you make your oven out of butter, I will donate it for free."

The Khelemites were ecstatic, until one of them shouted: "You must be crazy! The butter will melt in the fire!"

So the Khelemites reproached him: "You foolish man, would you rather freeze to death?"

At this point the Rebbe of Khelm stood up and pointed a finger at everybody: "Gentlemen! Don't be so hasty. We cannot make an oven out of butter, it's impossible."

"But why, Rebbe, why?" everybody wanted to know.

So the Rebbe replied:

"For the simple reason that when Friday night, the Eve of Sabbath arrives, and you are about to put a *Tcholnt* (a meat stew that cooks for twelve hours) into the oven . . . If the oven is *Milkhik* (dairy), you will have a *Treyfenem* (non-kosher) oven on your hands. Have you thought of that?"

כבוד

Hebrew—*Kavod*

Yiddish—*Koved*

Pride/Honor

Rebbe Mendele Lubavitcher used to say:
> *"The worst pride is the pride of being pious."*

Rebbe Naftali Rapshitser used to say:
> *"Do not wear an upper garment that consists of pride, the undergarment of rage, sewn with stitches of despair."*

It is said:
> *A non-believing Jew is also a Jew.*

It is also said:
> *A Jew who is a Torah Scholar cannot be a Hassid, and an ignorant Jew cannot be a Heretic.*

כאָלערע

Cholere

Cholera is a disease.

Yiddish Curses by Sholem Aleichem's Stepmother
by Sholem Aleichem

The Cholera should only get a hold of you, God in Heaven
The worms should eat you.
The leeches should drink your blood.
Shrounds should be sewn for you.
You should be silent forever.
The evil spirit should carry you on his shoulders.

Serab el Khadem
Sinai, Proto-Canaanite
1500 BCE

Proto-Canaanite
13th–12th BCE

Ahiram Sarcophagus
Phoenician
1000 BCE

Gezer Calendar
Hebrew
End of 10th century BCE

Mesha Stete
Hebrew Script
Mid 9th century BCE

Kilamu Inscription
Phoenician last third
of 9th century BCE

Siloam Inscription
Hebrew
late 8th century BCE

Hebrew Seals
7th century BCE

Hebrew Ostraca
Arad
early 6th century BCE

Elephantine Papyrus
Aramaic
Late 5th century BCE

Leviticus Scroll, Qumran
Paleo-Hebrew
Late 2nd century BCE

Samaritan Manuscript
13th century BCE

Isaiah Scroll I Qumran
Square Hebrew Script
Late 2nd century BCE

Classical Greek Script

Latin Script

Nabataean Script
1st century BCE

Classical
Arabic Script

ל Lamed

ל Lamed

Numeric Value of 13

Represents a stick to drive oxen

Also represents teaching, a symbol
of direction and conduct.

riginally the letter Lamed meant to prick, sting, incite, goad, as in the rod of a teacher. Because of its tall stature, the stern commandments in the Bible begin with the letter Lamed:

לא תרצח	לא תגנוב
Lo Tirtzakh	*Lo Tignov*
Thou shalt not murder.	Thou shalt not steal.

The Ben Zion Zuckerman letter Lamed (page 72) depicts a snake (in Yiddish a *Shlang)* who gave the Apple of the Tree of Knowledge—*Limud*—to Eve.

שלאַנג
Yiddish—*Shlang*
Snake

The Legend of the Snake

The cleverest of all the animals in the Garden of Eden was the snake, who stood on both legs like a camel and was envious that God was preparing a great feast for Adam and Eve. Eve was very beautiful, and the Snake was extremely jealous of the happy couple, so he decided to kill Adam and take Eve for himself. He sat down next to her and started a conversation: "Is it true, my dearest Eve, that you and Adam can eat the fruit of all the trees except for one?"

Eve demurely replied: "To tell you the truth, I think that Adam is a bit childish and he exaggerates a lot."

The Snake responded: "You, my dear, must know that God Himself eats the fruit from all the trees and when He is done, He creates worlds. It's very possible that He doesn't want you to eat from the Tree of Knowledge—you might also want to start creating worlds."

And then, the Snake grabbed Eve and threw her against the Tree of Knowledge. Then the snake began violently shaking the Tree and the fruit fell all around them. The Snake ate an apple and offered it to Eve, saying: "You see, you fell upon the Tree of Knowledge and were not harmed. I have eaten an apple and I have survived."

Eve bit into the fruit, and suddenly the Angel of Death appeared before her. She fearfully ran to Adam and offered him the fruit as well. Adam refused, and Eve got angry, shouting: "Do you think I will die before you, Adam, and that God will grant you a new Eve? At least let's die together and if we survive, let's survive together."

Adam ate the apple, and Eve made all the animals in Eden eat from the forbidden fruit, as well. Since then, all living creatures must die, except for one—the Phoenix—that didn't taste from the forbidden fruit and lives forever, resurrecting in the Holy flames of God.

Eve was punished with great pain at childbirth, and the Snake was forced to crawl on his stomach and eat the dirt around him for all eternity.

לילה	לילית
Layla	*Lilith*
Refers to Night	The first wife of Adam

It is said that while Adam was asleep, God bestowed upon him a female companion, his first wife, named Lilith, which came from the Hebrew word *Layla* that represents "night."

According to legend, they were attached to each other at the spine as Siamese twins. So Adam complained to God: "Father in Heaven, separate us for we are very unhappy and distraught."

So God put his palm through the spine of both Adam and Lilith and separated them. But this marital match didn't work. When it came to copulation, Lilith refused to lie underneath Adam—she wanted to be the one on top.

Once again Adam complained to God: "Dear God! You gave me a wife who is nothing but trouble, she doesn't obey, she has her own mind!"

And Lilith did have her own mind—she uttered God's name and flew off into the distance, leaving Adam alone and distraught. God called three angels and ordered them to find her, which they did, at the Red Sea, and ordered her to return to Adam.

She refused, saying: "Never! I don't love him and I don't need him!"

So Lilith became the "Sorceress" in our Jewish folklore: constantly pregnant, collecting the sperm of young men who masturbate, and giving birth to demons.

To confuse the wrath of Lilith, mothers would dress up their little boys in girl's dresses, letting their hair grow long, so that Lilith might mistake them for girls.

Once Lilith was gone, along came Eve—חוה (Khava)—who fed Adam the fruit of the Tree of Knowledge, and that's when he realized how insignificant he really was. Which brings us to the idea that the more we taste of the fruit of knowledge, the more we realize how little we know and how insignificant we are in comparison to the sea of knowledge.

ל	Serab el Khadem Sinai, Proto-Canaanite 1500 BCE
ע	Proto-Canaanite 13th–12th BCE
ℓ	Ahiram Sarcophagus Phoenician 1000 BCE
∠	Gezer Calendar Hebrew End of 10th century BCE
ℓ	Mesha Stete Hebrew Script Mid 9th century BCE
ℓ	Kilamu Inscription Phoenician last third of 9th century BCE
ℓ	Siloam Inscription Hebrew Late 8th century BCE
ℓ	Hebrew Seals 7th century BCE
L	Hebrew Ostraca Arad Early 6th century BCE
(	Elephantine Papyrus Aramaic Late 5th century BCE
∠	Leviticus Scroll, Qumran Paleo-Hebrew Late 2nd century BCE
ζ	Samaritan Manuscript 13th century BCE
ל	Isaiah Scroll I Qumran Square Hebrew Script Late 2nd century BCE
Λ	Classical Greek Script
L	Latin Script
J	Nabataean Script 1st century BCE
J	Classical Arabic Script

ליבע

Yiddish—*Libeh*

Love

A Love Letter from a Gentle Lady
by Yisroel Mayofes

One beautiful morning I received a love letter, written by a gentle lady's hand. The letter read as follows:

The person writing this letter is not known to you, but I must confess that I am terribly in love with you. Let me tell you about myself. I am young, pretty and picante. I have a number of admirers, but no one interests me since I saw you. I am desperate to meet with you, to get to know you better and express my deep love for you.

Meet me tomorrow, between eight and nine in the evening, in the White Rose restaurant. Please bring a white rose and order a bottle of Mumm champagne. That is how I will recognize you.

We will drink the champagne and spend a delightful evening together. I am overjoyed at the very prospect of our rendezvous.

Yours,
Johanna

I read the letter several times and decided to visit the White Rose to meet this intriguing and daring young Johanna. I dressed up in my best suit, bought a bouquet of white roses, and exactly at eight o'clock, I was in the restaurant ordering the Mumm champagne.

I waited for her with great trepidation and excitement.

Time passed, the clock rang eight, nine and ten, and Johanna didn't show up. I waited another hour, drank the entire bottle of champagne, and finally went home, full of anger and resentment.

Since then I have discovered that the gentle lady's love letter was written by none other than the owner of the restaurant, who was sending letters to unsuspecting men in order to sell his surplus Mumm champagne.

I could have been furious, but instead I realized that the few hours I spent in anticipation of a glorious love affair was well worth the price of my evening at the White Rose.

ל׳ו Lamed Vov

Numeric Value of 36

Represents the 36 Righteous Jews that allow the world to survive

מ Mem

בן־ציון צוקערמאַן

ם Mem Sofit

מ Mem   ם Mem Sofit

Final Mem—at the end of a word

Numeric Value of 40

Represents מים—*Mayim*—Water/fluid,
also a symbol for work, function,
womb, motherhood, and fruitfulness.

By virtue of the letter מ, the Jews ate מן "manna" in the desert for forty years.

The Zohar—the mystic Book of Splendor—associates the cryptic letter מ with the symbol of death, because of the Hebrew word מות—*Mavet* (Death).

Legend has it that when Adam was about to eat the fruit from the עץ הדעת—*Ets Hadaat*, the forbidden Tree of Knowledge, the letter מ—Mem hovered over him while searching for his companions, the letter Vav and the letter Tav, which make up the word *Mavet*—"death."

That was the first time that death appeared on earth.

> מזוזה
> Hebrew—*Mezuzah*
> Yiddish—*Mezuzeh*

The Mezuzah is a small tube attached to the outside doorpost containing an inscribed strip of parchment with Torah passages, it acts as a magic spell that wards off the evil spirit.

Observant Jews kiss the Mezuzah upon entering or leaving any Jewish house. Pious Jews also believe that if disaster strikes, you must check the Mezuzah for any damaged letters in the inscription.

Mezuzahs are also worn as lockets around the neck.

A "Mezuzah" Story:

A Reform Jew pours out his heart to the rabbi:

"My son has become very Orthodox, he goes to a Yeshivah (a Hebrew Academy for boys) full time and claims that everything in our house is *Treyf*, not kosher, so now he can never eat with us. Worst of all, he has now influenced our daughter, who has left our house and gone to study at some ultra-Orthodox seminary for women in Jerusalem."

The rabbi asks: "What about your youngest son, the one who went to Harvard?"

The father replies: "He has also become very orthodox. He hooked up with some Hassidim and he lives in a Yeshivah in Brooklyn."

The Reform rabbi was at a loss, until he shouted out triumphantly: "Listen, have you thought of checking your Mezuzah?"

משוגעת
Yiddish—*Mishigas*
Craziness; Insanity

Sam Levinson, the brilliant American humorist once said:

"Insanity and meshugas is genetic—
you can inherit it from your own children."

Sam Levinson, humorist

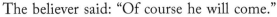

משיח

Meshiyakh

Messiah

Before Reb Yisroel Baalshem-Tov passed away, he called his disciples and said to them: "I want you to know that the Messiah will not come to redeem the Jews from their exile until the spirit of the Khassidism will penetrate deeply into the minds and hearts of the Jewish masses."

Three men were debating among themselves whether the Messiah would ever come.

The believer said: "Of course he will come."

The agnostic said: "I don't know; maybe he will and maybe he won't."

The heretic said: "There is no messiah, just as there is no God."

But when the messiah does come, the believer will say: "You see! I told you he'd come."

The agnostic will say: "So he came after all."

And the heretic will say:

"קוים מיט צרות זיך דערשלעפט מזל טוב!"

"Koym mit tsores zikh dershlept…"

"Look at how long it took him! Mazl-Tov!"

Ashmeday

Ashmeday, the Angel of Death, stems from Persia. His name is known in the old Persian belief—he is named as Ashmah Daedah. Ashmah is their god, and Daedah is full of wrath and lies. In the *Book of Tuviah*, which was written in Greek, the Devil is known as Asmadeus. It is said in the Book of Ecclesiastes (Kohelet) that Ashmeday had turned himself into King

Solomon, banished King Solomon from his throne, and sat himself on the King's throne, pretending to be the king. As the good book tells, King Solomon was wandering through the streets of Jerusalem, dressed in rags shouting, "I am King Solomon," but no one paid any attention until they discovered that the Ashmeday was sitting on the king's throne. So they banished him and put King Solomon back on his throne.

Proverbs About the Angel of Death

As superstition has its own logic, the Jews invented a treasury of proverbs regarding the Angel of Death. Among them:

The Angel of Death slaughters and remains in the right.

In a house of a sick man, the Angel of Death walks around.

When it thunders, it's a sign that some demons are being killed in Heaven.

One of our curses says: "The Angel of Death should fall in love with him or her."

In the town of fools, Khelm, the foolish people didn't know where old age came from, so they speculated that it came from afar. They decided to build a tower around their town of Khelm, and when they saw that it did't help, they decided to burn the Calendar with all the dates, until they realized that old age was smuggled in by the Angel of Death.

It is also said that the first gray hair is a notice from the Angel of Death, so with a tone of resignation we say: "Gray hair are the flowers of graves."

It is also said that you can rely on the Angel of Death; he is punctual.

מ	
	Serab el Khadem Sinai, Proto-Canaanite 1500 BCE
	Proto-Canaanite 13th–12th BCE
	Ahiram Sarcophagus Phoenician 1000 BCE
	Gezer Calendar Hebrew End of 10th century BCE
	Mesha Stete Hebrew Script Mid 9th century BCE
	Kilamu Inscription Phoenician last third of 9th century BCE
	Siloam Inscription Hebrew Late 8th century BCE
	Hebrew Seals 7th century BCE
	Hebrew Ostraca Arad Early 6th century BCE
	Elephantine Papyrus Aramaic Late 5th century BCE
	Leviticus Scroll, Qumran Paleo-Hebrew Late 2nd century BCE
	Samaritan Manuscript 13th century BCE
	Isaiah Scroll I Qumran Square Hebrew Script Late 2nd century BCE
M	Classical Greek Script
M	Latin Script
	Nabataean Script 1st century BCE
	Classical Arabic Script

The Story of the Town Preacher

There appeared in the city of Vilna in Lithuania a new *Magid*, a town preacher, who annoyed the town trustees to no end.

They contended: "Is it not enough that we ourselves have no livelihood to speak of, this preacher may take the bread out of our own mouths."

The new preacher wasn't discouraged: "Don't fret. I will tell you a parable, so pay heed to what I have to say.

"Once a woman was in possession of a great big chicken coop. Days went by and she would forget to feed the chickens. One plain Monday, the woman bought a rooster and threw him into the chicken coop. It so happens that a rooster is not a hen, he demands to be fed, he crows loudly and makes a fuss demanding his due. As soon as the woman heard the rooster crow and carry on without a stop, she remembered that she needed to feed the chickens.

"The same applies to me, as long as you were all alone in town, you were forgotten, but now, since I am here, I will preach until the city will wake up and acknowledge our presence, and from that moment on we will live in affluence and joy."

Sholem Yankev Abramowicz,
aka Mendele the Book Seller

מענדעלע מוכר ספרים

Hebrew—*Mendele Mokher Sfarin*
Yiddish—*Mendele Moykher Sforim*
Sholem Yankev Abramowicz (1836–1917)

Born in Kapulye in White Russia, he is known as the grandfather of modern Yiddish literature.

He once said: "If I were a rich man, I would establish rooms in different cities. My office in London, my dining room in Paris, and my guest room in Vienna."

נ Nun

Nun Sofit

נ Nun | Nun Sofit

Final Nun—at the end of a word

Numeric Value of 50

Represents Fish

---

un represents fish, symbol for reproduction. It symbolizes living creatures that multiply at great speed, propagation, sperm, offspring, and all the coming generations.

Chaim Vital, the mystic, put a damper on the letter Nun, only because it begins the words נחש *Nakhash* (serpent) and נפילה *Nefila* (the fallen), words of low esteem.

Noah, on the other hand, was the savior of the generation after the flood, and was about to be appointed as the redeemer of the Jewish exile, but he couldn't accomplish his mission only because the letter Nun in Noah took up such a central position in his name.

Would his name have been reversed and spelled instead of נח *Noakh*—חן— *Khen*, meaning charm, Khayim Vital says, the Jews would have been redeemed ages ago.

The *Khanukah-Dreydl*, or top, is adorned with four letters:

נ ג ה ש
Nun, Giml, Hey, Shin

The Dreydl game is played with the following rules:

> *Nun/Nisht* = None
> *Giml/Gut* = Good
> *Hey/Halb* = Half
> *Shin/Shlekht* = No good, or bad, put up

Interesting to note that the top twirl/spinning game can also be found among other nations using the Latin letters A—T—N—D: *Aufer* (take); *Totum* (all); *Nihili* (nothing); *Depone* (put in)

> נשמה
> Hebrew—*Neshama*
> Yiddish—*Neshomeh*
> Soul, from the Hebrew *Neshimah*—Breath

The Tricks, a Legend

In the town of Medzhibozh, in Poland, where the Baal Shem Tov, the great rabbi known as the Master of the Good Name lived and died, a group of acrobats, circus people, and contortionists (who performed tricks with their bodies) came to town. They pulled a rope across the river, and one of them walked across it without falling.

People were running to see the wonders of these performing acrobats, and along came the Baal Shem Tov to see the amazing feat. His students were amazed to see the rabbi among them and asked him why he had left his studies to observe this curiosity.

He responded: "I came to observe how a man walks across a deep abyss and I thought to myself, if only man could work so hard to repair his *neshome*, his soul, how many deep crevices he would have to overcome."

This expression originated in the Ukraine. The Ukrainians used to point at the Jews and say: "*Nye Bokha*," which means, "Here come the people who don't believe in our God."

נאַר ־ נאַראָנים

Yiddish—*Nar; Naronim*

Fool; fools

Once Rabbi Ayzil Slonimer was asked: "In your opinion, what percentage of wise men do the Jewish people account for?"

He replied: "Not more than ten percent."

"How did you come to that conclusion?" they wanted to know.

He replied: "It seems that Moses himself stated that he took only the tenth man, namely a wise man, on his journey to recover the Holy Land, on account that every tenth man was wise."

The people wanted to know how many fools do the Jews account for.

His answer was: "According to my calculation, not less than ten percent of fools."

The people wanted to know how he came to that conclusion, to which he replied: "Very simple! I deduce it from the number of cantors, for they make up only one of every ten at every quorum."

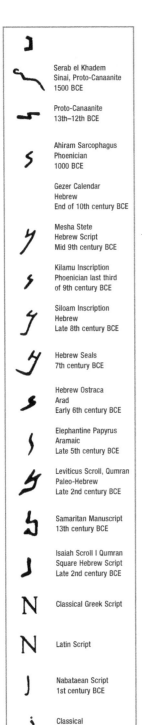

Serab el Khadem
Sinai, Proto-Canaanite
1500 BCE

Proto-Canaanite
13th–12th BCE

Ahiram Sarcophagus
Phoenician
1000 BCE

Gezer Calendar
Hebrew
End of 10th century BCE

Mesha Stete
Hebrew Script
Mid 9th century BCE

Kilamu Inscription
Phoenician last third
of 9th century BCE

Siloam Inscription
Hebrew
Late 8th century BCE

Hebrew Seals
7th century BCE

Hebrew Ostraca
Arad
Early 6th century BCE

Elephantine Papyrus
Aramaic
Late 5th century BCE

Leviticus Scroll, Qumran
Paleo-Hebrew
Late 2nd century BCE

Samaritan Manuscript
13th century BCE

Isaiah Scroll I Qumran
Square Hebrew Script
Late 2nd century BCE

Classical Greek Script

Latin Script

Nabataean Script
1st century BCE

Classical
Arabic Script

נאָמען
Yiddish—*Nomen*
Name

The Frankfurter Story

Stanley Frankfurter went down to the courthouse to change his name.

The judge asked him: "Why do you want to change your name? I don't see anything wrong with Frankfurter."

Stanley replied: "Well, you see judge, I want my name to sound real American, I want to blend in with the crowd."

The judge asked: "What do you want to call yourself now?"

Frankfurter's reply: "I decided to change my name to Wiener."

The Legend of Crazy Zelig

In the small town of Shavel, in prewar Poland, lived Zelig; everybody called him Crazy Zelig, or Meshugener Zelig.

Whenever he was lucid, people would ask him: "Zeylig! Where does your insanity come from?"

Zelig would recall this story:

"It might sound crazy to you, but I believe there is a God in Heaven and He sends down a little bundle of troubles for each one of us. Some of us get a bundle of joy, some get barrels of pleasure from their children, while others get a full bundle of heartache.

"As far as I am concerned, God has sent me a great bundle full of joy and pleasure. The only problem is that it fell on my head."

o Samekh

o **Samekh**

Numeric Value of 60

To depend on

The letter O Samekh looks more like an English O, closed on all sides, and is said to carry within it the secret of our Jewish exile.

It also represents a serpent that holds its tail between its teeth. Jewish mystics refer to the concept of the closed figure as the symbol of God's Infinity.

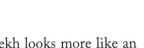

ספֿרדישע מעשה
A Sephardic Story

The Fable of the One-Eyed Donkey

A Yemenite Jew who lived in Sana, the Capital City of Yemen, described the difficult life for the Jews in Yemen. Government officials considered themselves the anointed masters of the Jews.

When a father of a Jewish family passed away, the son was immediately converted to Islam so that not a sign of their Jewish heritage should remain. The Jewish quarter of Sana, called Kav al Yahud, served as a sanctuary for the Jewish orphans. Here they lived and studied the Torah.

One day, a Kabil, a city official, discovered the class of Jewish boys studying with their rabbi.

"Who are these children?" the evil man demanded to know.

"Are you blind?" the rabbi replied. "Don't you see that these are not children. Some time ago they were all donkeys, but as soon as they studied the Torah, they became genuine children."

When the children heard what the rabbi said, they began howling and braying like donkeys. The rabbi went on: "As long as they study, they remain children."

The Kabil was convinced and turned to the rabbi with a request: "I and my wife have no children, but I do have a one-eyed donkey at home. Tomorrow I will bring him to you, and you will turn him into a boy."

The rabbi agreed, knowing full well he had fallen into a trap.

"I will give you three years," said the Kabil, "to turn my one-eyed donkey into a little boy."

Next day the Kabil brought his one-eyed donkey to the rabbi and reminded him that he would return in three years to collect his son.

The rabbi gave the donkey to another Kabil and forgot about it.

Three years passed, and the Kabil appeared demanding to see his little boy.

The rabbi said: "You know, your donkey was a genius—he learned the Torah so fast that he was appointed as the judge in the town of Demar."

The rabbi had remembered that the judge in Demar was blind in one eye, so the rabbi sent him there to find his son.

The minute the Kabil arrived in Demar, he went to the courthouse immediately. He found the one-eyed judge, embraced him with both hands and with tears in his eyes he cried out: "Don't you recognize me, my child, you used to be my one-eyed donkey."

The judge immediately ordered the crazy Kabil to be bound and chained.

The Kabil cried out: "This is how you thank your father? I should have left you the way you were, a donkey. At least then you would have been some help to me."

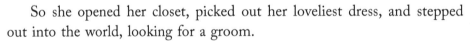

סאָשע דוואָשע

Sosheh Dvosheh

The Tiny Little Mouse

The Legend of the Little Mouse

Once there lived a tiny little mouse in a tiny little house and her name was Sosheh Dvosheh. She wore a tiny little dress, never a mess, but always out to impress.

As time went by, her mother, Mameleh, said to her: "The time has come for you to start looking for a groom. Your time is running out, but don't worry, I will call a matchmaker and he will bring grooms to choose from. All you'll have to do is pick one."

And so, the matchmaker brought a parade of grooms, but none of them were to Sosheh Dvosheh's liking.

One was handsome, but his whiskers were too long.

One was rich, but he couldn't even sign his name.

One was smart, but very, very naughty.

One was schooled but much too old.

Not one of them pleased Sosheh Dvosheh.

She wanted to marry someone special, extraordinary, someone she could love till the end of days.

Someone who could share her tiny little mouse house.

So she opened her closet, picked out her loveliest dress, and stepped out into the world, looking for a groom.

And when she lifted her eyes up to the sky, she saw the sun and fell in love. She just knew that the sun would make a perfect groom for her, and she called out: "Won't you marry me, Sun? We'll live happily ever after in my little mouse house."

Said the sun: "I am flattered you chose me to be your groom, but who am I compared to the cloud that covers my face every time he passes by."

Well, if that's the case, thought the mouse, *the cloud would make a perfect groom.*

She ran off looking for the cloud, and found him floating in the air, gazing lazily into the water.

"Won't you marry me, dearest cloud, and we'll live happily ever after in my mouse house?"

"I am flattered you chose me to be your groom," said the cloud, "but who am I compared to the wind that can carry me off to the end of the world. He lifts big ocean waves, tears out trees by their roots, and scatters their leaves all over town."

"Then the wind shall be a perfect groom for me!" cried out the mouse full of joy.

She ran off in search of the wind. Once she reached the open fields, she found the wind dancing and prancing among the flowers and tall grasses.

"Won't you marry me, windy wind, and we'll live happily for ever and ever in my mouse house."

The wind replied: "What good am I if a big tower stands in my way and doesn't let me pass?"

"Then the big tower would make a perfect groom for me," cried out the little mouse full of joy, and off she ran in search of the big tower.

And there he stood, majestic and proud of himself.

"Won't you marry me, you beautiful tower, and we'll live happily ever after in my mouse house."

Said the tower: "What good am I if a little mouse can dig up the very foundation I am built on."

If that's the case, thought the little mouse, *I had better find the little mouse, for he is the strongest of them all.*

And there he was, in all his mousy splendor. She winked and she blinked and she said to him: "Won't you marry me, mister mouse, and we will live happily ever after?"

And so they did. And to this day, the little mouse tells her tiny little mice children how she found the groom of her dreams.

Serab el Khadem
Sinai, Proto-Canaanite
1500 BCE

Proto-Canaanite
13th–12th BCE

Ahiram Sarcophagus
Phoenician
1000 BCE

Gezer Calendar
Hebrew
End of 10th century BCE

Mesha Stete
Hebrew Script
Mid 9th century BCE

Kilamu Inscription
Phoenician last third
of 9th century BCE

Siloam Inscription
Hebrew
Late 8th century BCE

Hebrew Seals
7th century BCE

Hebrew Ostraca
Arad
Early 6th century BCE

Elephantine Papyrus
Aramaic
Late 5th century BCE

Leviticus Scroll, Qumran
Paleo-Hebrew
Late 2nd century BCE

Samaritan Manuscript
13th century BCE

Isaiah Scroll I Qumran
Square Hebrew Script
Late 2nd century BCE

Classical Greek Script

Latin Script

Nabataean Script
1st century BCE

Classical
Arabic Script

ע Ayin

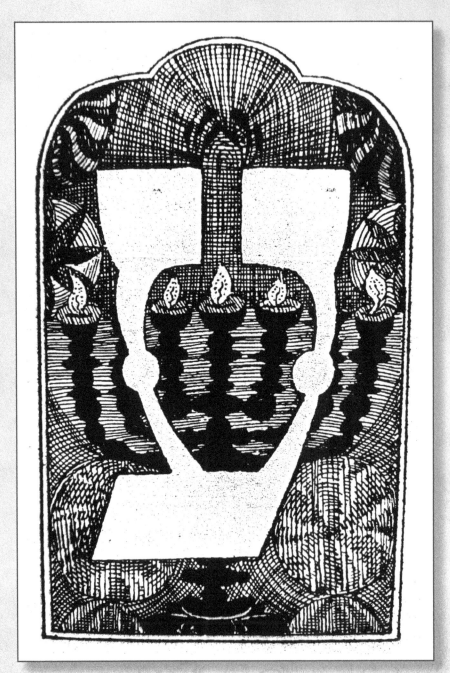

ע Ayin

Numeric Value of 70

The sound of the letter Ayin is Eh

Hebrew—עין—*Ayin* means Eye

Also Prophecy and Source

The letter Ayin—ע—symbolizes matter, whose attributes are appearance, surface, firmament, form, and color. It also represents the Eye of the Creator. The mystics believe in the concept that the Torah was conceived in God's Eyes before creation took place.

The geometric lines of the Ayin—ע—allude to infinity and the philosophic definition of God, whose center is everywhere and circumference nowhere

הקדוש ברוך הוא
Hakadosh Barukh Hu
Blessed be His Name

Legend has it that the Ayin—ע—came before God and said: "Would You create the world with me? After all, it's written, 'The eyes of God hover over the whole world.'"

To which God replied: "I will not create the world with you."

"Why?" asked the Ayin downcast.

And the answer came: "Because of the *Aveyra*, Sin—בעל־עבירה—the sinner. As it is written: 'The eye of the sinner awaits the dusk.'"

Dejected, the Ayin was turned away.

עברית

Hebrew—*Ivrit*

Hebrew

The Hebrew language began with the fusing of Canaanite, Accadien, Phoenician, Assyrian, Arabic, and Egyptian, which fused with Jewish Aramaic. In 612 BCE, Hebrew further fused with Persian dialects.

In Babylonia, during our first exile, Hebrew ceased to be spoken completely by 586 BCE.

עברות

Hebrew—*Aveyrot*

Yiddish—*Aveyres*

Sins; Transgressions

A Yiddish Story

When a Jew in the shtetl got sick with fever and the shakes, he went to a doctor.

The doctor told him that he had been infected with "a virus."

The man couldn't understand, saying: "But *Avayres* (instead of a virus) are bad deeds. I may not do too many *Mitsves* (good deeds), but my *Avayres* couldn't be that bad . . ."

עין הרע

Hebrew—*Ayin Hara*

Yiddish—*Ayne Horeh*

The Evil Eye

The Evil Eye—A Superstition

To ward off the evil eye, Jews and many other ethnic groups spit three times, *Tfu! Tfu! Tfu!*

The superstitious believe in the evil eye, which has existed since before Talmudic times. Evil eye incantations say that the evil eye is a terrible disease, and the Talmud brings all kinds of spells to avoid it, including amulets, ancient remedies, and medications to heal it.

קיין עין הרע
Yiddish—*Kayn ain horeh*
No evil eye

A Yiddish Story

A Jewish tourist goes to Ireland. He visits a synagogue and asks one of the worshippers:

"?נו, וואָס הערט זיך עפעס נײַעס אין גלאָקקאַ מאָראַ"
"Nu, vos hert zikh epes nayes in Glocca Morra?"
"So, what's new in Glocca Morra?"

And he was told:

"זייער גוט קיין עין הרע"
"Zeyer gut kayn eyne hore!"
"Very well, with no evil eye!"

◁•▷

The Talmud says that when a stranger comes into a town, he should fear the evil eye, since he knows that people are afraid of strangers and look upon them with suspicion.

The stranger should put one finger of his right hand into his left fist, and one finger of his left hand into his right fist and say: "I, Ployni ben Ployni, the anonymous son of an anonymous son, stem from Patriarch Joseph's children and the evil eye has no power over me."

A Little Jewish Humor

Customer: "Hello, Yankl, how is the butcher business? I see *Kayn Eyne Hore,* no evil eye, *Tfu! Tfu! Tfu!* Now tell me, Yankl, do you have any fresh meat today?"

Yankl: "I have only rotten meat today! I deliberately pick up rotten meat for my customers, so if you want rotten meat, you can have it. When I was in the slaughterhouse today I said: 'Make sure you give me rotten meat because only some people like fresh meat.'"

Serab el Khadem
Sinai, Proto-Canaanite
1500 BCE

Proto-Canaanite
13th–12th BCE

Ahiram Sarcophagus
Phoenician
1000 BCE

Gezer Calendar
Hebrew
End of 10th century BCE

Mesha Stete
Hebrew Script
Mid 9th century BCE

Kilamu Inscription
Phoenician last third
of 9th century BCE

Siloam Inscription
Hebrew
Late 8th century BCE

Hebrew Seals
7th century BCE

Hebrew Ostraca
Arad
Early 6th century BCE

Elephantine Papyrus
Aramaic
Late 5th century BCE

Leviticus Scroll, Qumran
Paleo-Hebrew
Late 2nd century BCE

Samaritan Manuscript
13th century BCE

Isaiah Scroll I Qumran
Square Hebrew Script
Late 2nd century BCE

Classical Greek Script

Latin Script

Nabataean Script
1st century BCE

Classical
Arabic Script

פ Pey

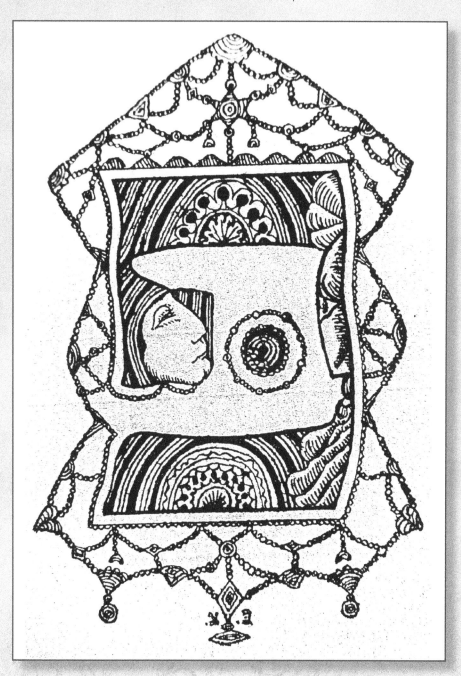

פ Fey

ר   Fey Sofit

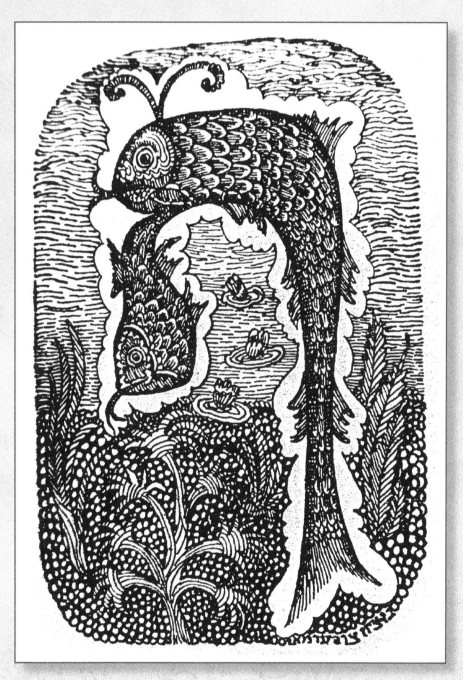

פ Pey פ Fey
ף Fey Sofit

Final Fey—at the end of a word

Numeric Value of 80

Pey—P sound   Fey—F sound

Represents פה

Hebrew—*Peh*—Mouth

The letters Pey פ and Fey פ also stand for language.

It is said that the *Shekhina* (the Divine Presence) underwent *Tsim-Tsum* (Contraction). In the Kabbalah, God undergoes self-contraction to allow room for creation, miraculously making His *Mishkan* sanctuary in the letters Fey and Pey.

It is also a graphic scheme of body and soul.

> י.ל. פרץ
> Yitzkhok Leib Peretz
> A Classic Yiddish Writer

THE STRANGER
By I. L. Peretz

There once was a stranger who lived in a village where no one spoke his language. One day the stranger found a diamond—it was shiny and glowed like the sun. He realized it must be worth a fortune, but that he would not be safe with his valuable discovery. He had to hide the diamond and not share this treasure—even with his wife.

So he went into his garden and buried his diamond near his home, and as a marker, he placed a large boulder on top of the spot. When better times arrive, he imagined, and there will be no more envy or hatred among neighbors and strangers, he will know where to find his treasure.

One day, his wife noticed the boulder and decided to use the spot to plant onions in its stead. She couldn't move the boulder by herself so she called her husband to help her.

Yitzkhok Leib Peretz, classic Yiddish writer

The husband shouted: "God forbid, don't touch that stone!"

"Why?" asked his wife.

Frightened, the husband replied: "This is our lucky stone, it brings us blessings and joy."

She was not sure whether her husband was joking or not, but she decided that this was an omen from Heaven.

Next day, the husband sees two boulders on the same spot in the garden and asks his wife: "Why is there a second boulder here?"

His wife smiles and says: "I couldn't sleep last night. I realized that two is better than one, so I got out of bed and added another stone."

The couple had two children, a boy and a girl, who did everything her mother did. When the mother placed large stones on the spot, the daughter placed small rocks.

Their clever son wanted to know why there were so many rocks in the garden.

His mother said: "It brings us luck."

He asked his father what it meant, and his father said: "When you get older, you'll understand."

When his son grew up, his father told him about the secret treasure buried under the stones, so that in every generation only one person would know about the diamond, while everyone else thought that rocks were lucky.

As the generations have passed, the diamond has been forgotten and people continue to fight over stones.

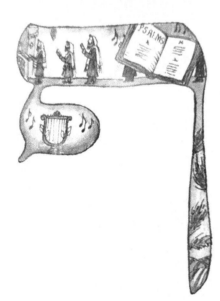

BUT PRAY WE MUST

By I. L. Peretz

Berl the tailor was overjoyed to finally see his son the doctor; he wanted to take him to the synagogue to pray.

"I'm not going!" said the doctor.

"Are you ashamed of me?" asked the father.

"God forbid," replied the son.

"Now that you are a doctor, do you no longer have to praise God?" the father responded.

"That's not it, Father."

"What is it then?" the father wanted to know.

"How can I explain this?" asked the son. "How would you like it if someone kept on telling you what a good tailor you are—a great tailor, an honest tailor, a one and only tailor."

"What are you talking about?" asked the father.

"Father, God is much wiser than we are," replied the son. "Do you think he needs our praise? Great God, Honest God, One and Only God?"

The father thought for a moment and replied: "You are absolutely right, Son, but pray we must."

<table>
<tr><td style="text-align:center">פורים
Purim
Holiday</td></tr>
</table>

Purim Stories

On Purim, the Jews were saved.

More than two thousand years ago, King Akhashveyrosh (Ahasverus) of Persia was looking for a new bride, and a beauty contest was prepared. The king would marry the most beautiful woman in the kingdom.

A Jewish girl named Esther had an uncle whose name was Mordekhay, and he convinced Esther to participate. She was chosen as the new queen.

The king had a minister by the name of Haman, who hated the Jews and was plotting to kill them. Mordekhay found out and pleaded with Esther to inform the king of the impending plot.

The king ordered wicked Haman to be hung while Mordekhay was paraded through the city riding on a horse.

Purim is a happy holiday: we read *M'gilas Esther*, the Scroll of Esther, the only biblical chapter in which God is never mentioned. We are encouraged to celebrate and get drunk until we can't tell the difference between Esther's blessed Uncle Mordekhay and the cursed Prime Minister Haman who wanted to kill all Jews.

On Purim, in the year 1524, another story of a plot to kill Jews took place in Cairo, Egypt.

The Sultan Suleiman II was the governor at that time and his deputy was a despotic Jew hater. He arrested many Jews and threw them into jail while plotting to kill all the Jews of Egypt.

On the day of the proposed executions, a miracle occurred. An uprising broke out against the governor and his own people decapitated him.

Another story, called "Purim Vints," occurred on Purim in the seventeenth century in the city of Frankfurt, Germany.

The economic conditions at that time in Germany were devastating, and the Jews were accused of causing the financial disaster. The provocateur calling for the destruction of the Jews was Vintsents, or "Vints" Hans Fetmilch. In the year 1614, he organized a pogrom on the Jewish ghetto. Jewish homes were robbed, and the Jews were chased out of the city.

When the German king found out, he arrested Fetmilch together with his cohorts.

On Purim day, they were hanged. The Jews of Frankfurt all returned, the king paid for all their damages, and the German Jewish community celebrated "Purim Vints" every year until the nineteenth century.

Purim Customs

Jews use gragers, noisemakers, to make noise when-ever Haman's name is mentioned in the Megilah.

There was also a custom among Jews to write Haman's name on the soles of their shoes and jump up and down.

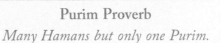

> ### Purim Proverb
> *Many Hamans but only one Purim.*

The Passover Holiday

After Purim, Jews get ready to celebrate Passover, the holiday of freedom. Wine was made out of raisins and stored, and the bakeries worked overtime.

Everyone went to the baker with their bag of flour to order matza to be made. The rabbi and some of his influential town's people would go from house to house to collect money to purchase matza for the poor.

The children are taught to read the Haggadah, the story of Passover, with explanations.

During Passover, Jews retell the story of slavery in the land of Egypt, the evil King Pharaoh and how Moses led them to freedom.

Traditionally at the Passover Seder ceremony, the youngest child recites the four questions:

1. *Ma nishtano halaylah haze mikol haleylot?* (Why is this night different from all other nights?) On all other nights we eat both *khomets* leavened bread and matza, but on this Passover night—only matza.

2. On all other nights we eat all sorts of vegetables, but on this night we eat *morer*—bitter herbs.

3. On all other nights we do not dip even once, but on this night we dip twice, once *karpas* greenery and salt water, and once in *morer* and *kharoyses*—bitter herbs and brown sweet paste, prepared with apples, nuts, spices and wine, as a reminder of the clay when Jews in Egypt made bricks.

4. On all other nights we can sit both upright and reclining, but on this Passover night we sit reclining, to celebrate freedom from slavery.

𐤐	
	Serab el Khadem Sinai, Proto-Canaanite 1500 BCE
	Proto-Canaanite 13th–12th BCE
	Ahiram Sarcophagus Phoenician 1000 BCE
	Gezer Calendar Hebrew End of 10th century BCE
	Mesha Stete Hebrew Script Mid 9th century BCE
	Kilamu Inscription Phoenician last third of 9th century BCE
	Siloam Inscription Hebrew Late 8th century BCE
	Hebrew Seals 7th century BCE
	Hebrew Ostraca Arad Early 6th century BCE
	Elephantine Papyrus Aramaic Late 5th century BCE
	Leviticus Scroll, Qumran Paleo-Hebrew Late 2nd century BCE
	Samaritan Manuscript 13th century BCE
	Isaiah Scroll I Qumran Square Hebrew Script Late 2nd century BCE
Π	Classical Greek Script
P	Latin Script
	Nabataean Script 1st century BCE
	Classical Arabic Script

Afikoman

Eliyahu Bokhur, the author of the *Bovo Bukh* (the *Book of Bovo d'Antuna*) in the sixteenth century, says that the Afikoman comes to us from the Greek—meaning festive occasion. It was the middle Matza, that was hidden, while children went looking for it. Once they found it, they received a gift.

The afikoman was also used as an amulet that a young girl would put under her pillow, hoping to become a bride.

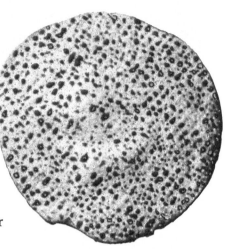

Jews were redeemed from Egypt because they didn't change their names, their language, and didn't abolish circumcision—Brit Milah.

A Story About Rabbi Israel Salanter

Founder of the nineteenth-century Jewish, religious Mussar movement and Mussar Yeshivot, put great emphasis on moral and ethical values.

Rabbi Israel Salanter

Before the Passover holiday, he would come to the bakery to supervise the women who kneaded and rolled the dough to bake the matza for Passover.

One week, before Passover holiday, the rabbi became ill and couldn't go to the bakery. The young Yeshivah boys, his followers, consoled him: "Tell us Rabbi, what is it that you want us to do?"

The rabbi explained carefully: "First and foremost I want you to watch the poor widows who knead and roll the dough to make the Matza. See to it that no one abuses them, mistreats them, nor is angry at them. The ritual of Matzo purity is indeed very important, but those that bake the holy Matzo are of utmost importance."

Ү Tsadik Sofit

צ Tsadik   ץ Tsadik Sofit

Final Tsadik—at the end of a word

Numeric Value of 90

TZ sound

Hebrew—Tsadi   Yiddish—Tsadik

It represents a Fishing Rod

---

he word *Tsadik* refers to a single righteous and charitable man, while *Tsadikim* refers to a number of righteous man. Our folklore introduces us to the Lamed Vov Tsadikim, thirty-six righteous men who hold up the world with their charity and goodness.

> צדיק
> Hebrew—*Tsadi*
> A Righteous Man

It is said that our biblical prophet Elijah sometimes comes down to earth disguised as one of the thirty-six Tsadikim in order to help out a needy family. Disguised as a peasant, he brings wood for the fireplace to keep the family warm, or food to feed the hungry.

Elijah the biblical prophet is considered a true *Tsadik*.

> צדקה
> Hebrew—*Tsedakah*
> Yiddish—*Tsedokeh*
> Charity

Jews have always been a charitable people. In the Eastern European shtetlekh, they supported poor brides (*Hakhnoses Kaleh*) or welcomed strangers and guests (*Hakhnoses Orkhim*) or the *Hekdesh*, the holy abode, connected to the synagogue in town where poor and homeless people were allowed to spend the night.

A Legend

Many years ago, before the First World War, there were many poor Jews wandering around Eastern Europe, from country to country, begging. Some poor Yeshivah students used to visit the courtyards where Jews lived and shout: "Throw down a Yeshivah boy from the second floor!"

The residents would throw their small change wrapped in newspaper in order to support the Torah studies of the poor students.

In the modern world, Jews are known as significant philanthropists, supporting major Jewish and non-Jewish institutions, including hospitals, universities, museums, and the arts.

צִיצִית
Hebrew—*Tzitzit*
Yiddish—*Tsitsis*

The word *Tzitzit* is Sumerian and Akkadian, and goes back to 22–24 BCE when the Royals used to wear "fringes" of gold and silver to display their riches, power, and superiority.

In time the Orthodox Jews imitated the royalty by wearing four tassels under their garments, connected to their prayer shawl, signifying a barrier between the holy and the profane.

The mystics assert that since the letter צ Tsadik follows the letter Kuf ק there must have been a strong attraction that gradually ended up in a merger forming the letter *Tsadik*, as we pronounce it in Yiddish.

In the Book of Splendor (the Zohar), it is observed that the Final Tsadik (ץ) is a symbol of a gallows, because it ends the word—עץ—Tree, where the sinners hang and the righteous are rewarded.

In Yiddish, a *Tsadik* also means a pious and righteous person—it is associated with the Peyresh "commentary":

Tsadik Yisod Olam
"The righteous are the foundation of the world."

A VIGNETTE
by Yiddish Humorist Moyshe Nadir (1885–1943)

For only ten cents, you can sit in an air-conditioned hall, listening to music or watching a film. You can see people torn apart, killed, and wounded, trains going off the tracks and exploding, ships sinking, and an assortment of other interesting misfortunes. All for ten cents.

So you turn to your wife and ask: "Would you like a piece of chocolate or a soft-drink? It's so delightfully cool here, maybe tomorrow we can set out on the ocean if the weather is good."

Serab el Khadem
Sinai, Proto-Canaanite
1500 BCE

Proto-Canaanite
13th–12th BCE

Ahiram Sarcophagus
Phoenician
1000 BCE

Gezer Calendar
Hebrew
End of 10th century BCE

Mesha Stete
Hebrew Script
Mid 9th century BCE

Kilamu Inscription
Phoenician last third
of 9th century BCE

Siloam Inscription
Hebrew
Late 8th century BCE

Hebrew Seals
7th century BCE

Hebrew Ostraca
Arad
Early 6th century BCE

Elephantine Papyrus
Aramaic
Late 5th century BCE

Leviticus Scroll, Qumran
Paleo-Hebrew
Late 2nd century BCE

Samaritan Manuscript
13th century BCE

Isaiah Scroll I Qumran
Square Hebrew Script
Late 2nd century BCE

Classical Greek Script

Latin Script

Nabataean Script
1st century BCE

Classical
Arabic Script

WE ARE ALL CONNECTED

by Moyshe Nadir

I am connected to my golden chain
Which is connected to my key
Which is connected to the door
Which is connected to the house
Which is connected to the foundation
Which is connected to the planet earth
Which is connected to the universe
Which is connected to God
Who is connected to eternity
Which is connected to itself

We are so terribly connected to our connections.
That we, in no way, want to disconnect ourselves.

ק Kof

ק **Kof**

Numeric Value of 100

Hebrew—Kof   Yiddish—Kuf

K sound

Represents the eye of a needle

---

he Kof symbolizes constant movement and politics, a sense of hearing, allusion, and the eye of a needle. It is also rooted in the word *Nakef*, the concept of bruising, beating, wounding, hurting, chopping, and cutting.

The letter Kuf has a blemish, because Cain's name starts with the letter ק Kuf— קין Kayin, Cain. The name Cain is so thoroughly entangled in Cain's original sin that it pursues Reb Chaim Vital, the Safed mystic, in his dreams, demanding that God clear the letter's name.

Because of its stern personality, the Kuf was appointed to serve as the policeman among the letters and entered into legend as the messenger of bad tidings and executor of Divine Wrath.

קידוש השם

Kidush Hashem

Sanctification of God's Name

It requires certain preparatory acts, as one must come before the Creator purified, with all the symbols of Judaism intact.

A True Story

The Jews of the West Galician town of Grodzisk sincerely believed that pious and God-fearing Jews must come to heaven with full beards and earlocks.

When the Nazis attacked their little town, they ordered all the Jewish men to shave off their beards and earlocks.

The Jews obeyed, hiding their beards and earlocks in their pockets, knowing that before being shot, they would be ordered to undress.

**Inscription on a wall in Cologne, Germany,
written by Jews hiding from the Germans:**

*I believe in the sun, though it shines not!
I believe in love, though I feel it not.
I believe in God even when He is silent.*

A Legend About King Solomon

The letter Kuf's greatest victim was Shlomo Hamelekh, King Solomon, known as the classic arbitrator.

The Zohar bases the tale on an old Midrash legend where King Solomon is brought to justice for breaking the ethical code of behavior.

As it is written:

לא ירבה לו סוסים
לא ירבה לו מאד נשים
לא ירבה לו מאד כסף וזהב

"You shall not multiply horses, women, silver, gold and much more." (Deut. 17), a bidding that King Solomon transgressed in great measure.

The letter Yud, the smallest letter of the Alef-Bet, was said to have represented King Solomon before the Celestial Court of Justice.

King Solomon lost his kingdom. It was God's verdict that Solomon vanish, but that his letter stay in its place and at that precise moment God's messenger, the letter Kuf, chased Solomon off his throne and turned him into a poor wandering beggar named Kohelet.

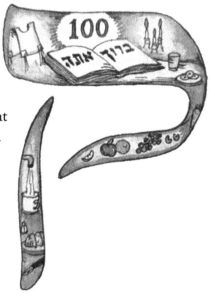

קהלת—Kohelet

Ecclesiastes

which represents:

קהל

Kahal

Community; Congregation; Society

As Kohelet roamed the four corners of the Earth, he called out:

אני קהלת

Ani Kohelet!

"I, Kohelet, was once King of Israel and Jerusalem."

Some mystics dwell on the interesting idea of a double personality for the letter Kuf that personifies both Solomon the King and Kohelet (Ecclesiates) the philosopher.

סיתרא אחרא

Sitra Akhra

The "Concealed Other" or the Evil Spirit;

the Devil

Excerpts from the Book of Ecclesiastes—Kohelet

"Vanity of Vanities," says Kohelet. "All is vanity!"

"For everything there is a time
And a time for everything under
the sun.
A time for being born
And a time to die
A time to plant
And a time to cut (during harvest)
A time to kill
And a time to heal
A time to destroy
And a time to build

A time to cry
And a time to laugh
A time to wail
And a time to dance
A time to be silent
And a time to speak
A time to love
And a time to hate
A time for war
And a time for peace!"

King Solomon—Kohelet—also is said to have written this love song:

שיר השירים

SHIR HASHIRIM

The Song of Songs

I hear the voice of my beloved
My beloved is like a gazelle
Like a young deer
My beloved called and said to me:
"Rise my love, my beauty,
Come away—
I am my beloved's
And he is mine—
Your very figure
Is like a palm-tree
Come, let us go into the fields...
There I will give my love to you...
Your breasts are like two fawns—
twins of a gazelle grazing among the lilies

The Rabbi of Prague (Folklore)

The Rabbi of Prague was once accosted by a madman who put a pistol to his head and shouted: "I want to see the Rabbi of Prague jump out of the second floor window and survive!"

The Rabbi of Prague listened to the demands of the madman and replied: "That is not a big *kunts,* everyone is capable of jumping from a second floor window, but the greater *kunts* would be if I go downstairs and jump up through the second floor window."

The madman agreed, and the Rabbi survived.

———⊲•⊳———

קוויטלעך
Yiddish—*Kvitlekh*
Little paper notes sent to God

Although our God sits up above, we know his address and we have access to Him. If we need him, we send him *Kvitlekh* with messengers, either to be delivered through the Wailing Wall in Jerusalem or through the services of a dead man, especially the intervention of a Holy Righteous man, a *Tsadik.*

Today there are online companies that provide this service.

קלאג מוטערס
Yiddish—*Klogmuters*
Wailing Mothers

The Mourners Fable

Wealthy Jews in the shtetl used to hire *Klogmuters*, wailing old women to mourn at their funerals. They not only cried but yelled and tore their hair out. The louder they screamed, the more money they would earn from the bereaved family.

קלוג
Klug
Smart

The Smartest Girl in the Land, a Legend

Once upon a time, long, long ago, there lived a nobleman who thought he was very smart. He had forests and windmills, horses and sheep, and a great big inn where his innkeeper sold wine and beer to the peasants.

The nobleman had many servants and having so much time on his hands, he liked to play games and tricks, but above all he liked to ask riddles that very few people could answer.

The nobleman had three favorite servants who ran his estate, one servant took care of the forest, the second took care of his windmills, and the third ran his inn.

One day he called all three of them and asked them three riddles, saying: Here are the riddles:

1. What is the fastest thing in the world?

2. What is the fattest thing in the world?

3. What is the most loved thing in the world?

"Those of you who can't answer these riddles will lose their position," the nobleman exclaimed, and left.

The keepers of the forests and the windmills conferred, and then agreed, exclaiming:

"The fastest thing in the world is the nobleman's horse! The fattest thing in the world is the nobleman's pig, and the most beloved thing in the world is the nobleman's mother."

Satisfied with their answers, they went home.

Only the innkeeper couldn't come up with an answer. He also went home. The innkeeper lived with his only daughter, who was not only the prettiest girl in the land but also the smartest. When she saw her father's sad face, she knew that something was making him unhappy.

"Tell me, Father," she said, "why do you look so worried?"

The father replied: "I'll tell you, my child. The nobleman asked us to solve three riddles. The other servants answered and happily went home, but I am very worried for I have no answers to the riddles."

"Don't you worry, dear Father, maybe I will be able to solve them."

After hearing the riddles, the daughter responded immediately: "The fastest thing in the world is an idea, the fattest thing in the world is the earth, and the thing that one loves best is sleep."

When all three servants came back with their answers, the nobleman dismissed the first two of them, but he liked the innkeeper's answers, asking him: "Tell me, who helped you with the answers?"

The innkeeper said: "It was my daughter who solved all your riddles."

"If that's the case," said the nobleman, "and if she is so smart, then let her come to meet me. I want to see her, but on one condition: she must come not walking and not riding, not dressed and not undressed, and bring me a present that is also not a present."

The innkeeper went home even more unhappy than before, but when his daughter saw his sad face she said: "You look worried, Father. Didn't the nobleman like your answers?"

The father replied: "He loved all your answers and wants to meet you right away, but with the stipulation that you come to his palace not walking and not riding, not dressed and not undressed, and with a present that is not a present."

The daughter smiled and comforted her father: "Don't you worry, Father. All I need you to do for me is go to the marketplace and buy me a fisherman's net, a donkey, a pair of turtledoves, and a pound of meat."

Puzzled the father replied: "What a funny combination of things you are asking for."

Once all the things that she requested were in place, the girl took off all her clothes and wrapped herself in the fisherman's net, this way she was not dressed and not undressed; she sat herself on the donkey with her feet dangling on the ground, so she wasn't walking, nor riding; she held both turtledoves in one hand and the pound of meat in the other; and this way she entered the nobleman's estate.

As she passed the gates, the nobleman's hound dogs tried to attack her, so she threw the pound of meat at them and they pounced on it, leaving her to enter the nobleman's estate.

When the nobleman arrived, she realized that he was very handsome and with a twinkle in her eyes, she said to him: "Noble lord, as you can see, I am wearing a fisherman's net, and I have entered riding a donkey with my feet on the ground, satisfying your first two riddles. For the third, I have brought you a gift, which is really not a gift," and she released the two turtledoves, who flew away through the open window.

The nobleman was amazed by her beauty and wisdom, and he said: "Since you are such a beautiful and clever girl, I shall marry you, but on one condition: you must promise never to try to solve any of my problems."

Serab el Khadem
Sinai, Proto-Canaanite
1500 BCE

Proto-Canaanite
13th–12th BCE

Ahiram Sarcophagus
Phoenician
1000 BCE

Gezer Calendar
Hebrew
End of 10th century BCE

Mesha Stete
Hebrew Script
Mid 9th century BCE

Kilamu Inscription
Phoenician last third
of 9th century BCE

Siloam Inscription
Hebrew
Late 8th century BCE

Hebrew Seals
7th century BCE

Hebrew Ostraca
Arad
Early 6th century BCE

Elephantine Papyrus
Aramaic
Late 5th century BCE

Leviticus Scroll, Qumran
Paleo-Hebrew
Late 2nd century BCE

Samaritan Manuscript
13th century BCE

Isaiah Scroll I Qumran
Square Hebrew Script
Late 2nd century BCE

Classical Greek Script

Latin Script

Nabataean Script
1st century BCE

Classical
Arabic Script

"You have my word," she replied, and married the nobleman.

One beautiful morning as she stood at the palace window, she saw a peasant crying hysterically.

"Why are you crying?" she wanted to know.

The peasant replied: "You see, noble lady, I own a barn together with my neighbor. I keep my mare at the far end of the barn, and he keeps his carriage on the other side. Yesterday, my mare gave birth to a little colt, right under my neighbor's carriage on the other side of the barn, so the neighbor claims that the little colt belongs to him. We went to your husband, the nobleman, for a judgment and he ruled in favor of my neighbor."

The nobleman's wife turned to the peasant and said: "Buy yourself a fishing rod and a sack of sand, spread the sand under the nobleman's window and pretend you are fishing. When the nobleman asks you what are you doing, you tell him that you are fishing. He will then ask you how you can catch fish standing on a pile of sand, and you will reply: 'If a carriage can give birth to a colt, I can catch fish on a pile of sand.'"

This is what the peasant did, and when the nobleman heard the answer, he knew that it had come from his wise and clever wife.

He became very, very angry and called out to her: "Since you broke your promise not to mix into my affairs, you can take the thing you love best and go back to your father's house!"

Said the nobleman's wife: "It would be my greatest pleasure to do as you ask, but before I go, we must drink to celebrate our parting of the ways."

The nobleman agreed. He drank one cup of wine after another until he fell asleep, and when he was fast asleep, his wife called the servants to help her put him into the coach and off they rode to her father's house. The next day, when the nobleman woke up, he realized he was in the house of his wife's father.

"What am I doing here?" he wanted to know.

His wife gently replied: "It was you who said to take the thing you love best and go to your father's house. I love you best, and so I took you."

ר Reysh

ר Reysh

Numeric Value of 200

The sound R

Aramaic—Reysh   Arabic—Ras

ictorially and literally, Reysh means *Rosh*, head. In old philosophical literature, the Reysh stood for psychic, instinctual, and mental remedies with the head at its center.

The Reysh symbolizes:

> די ירושה פֿון ישראל
> Yiddish—*Di Yerushe fun Yisroel*
> The Legacy of Israel

Also prosperity that is yet to come for the people of Israel.

The name of the first Jew was changed from אברם "father of Aram" to אברהם Avraham, "father of Hamon," or "Father of Nations."

Abraham undertook a new direction and a new mission.

Says Rashi: "As of now, his name should have been Avraham, condensed from אב המון, father of many." Still the letter Reysh remained in אברהם Avraham.

Thus, the answer is that the letter Reysh remained in Avraham because of its stubborn nature.

רפֿ׳אל
רפֿואל
Raphael the Healer
Represents Remedy

רפואה—Rfuah, the name, inspired the naming of the anticancer compound Refuin.

◁•▷

ראש השנה
Hebrew—*Rosh Hashana*
Yiddish—*Rosh Hashone*
Jewish New Year

A Legend About the Jewish New Year

Tisha B'Av—the ninth day of the twelfth month of the Jewish calendar, that falls around August—is a Jewish fast day.

It was customary in the shtetlekh, the small Eastern European towns, to visit the cemetery, the graves of their loved ones and pour out their bitter hearts and say prayers.

In case the women didn't know how to express their agony, they would hire a learned woman for this purpose.

From this day on, Jews begin to count toward their New Year. This is known as the *Sfira*, the "Counting."

In these little towns, there were also women who would take a ball of thread along with them, which they would use to measure the area of the cemetery, the graves of the holy rabbis and their family members.

They would later go to the wax-maker and order him to cut up the thread and make wicks for candles, which they donated to the synagogues.

During prayers, the candles were lit, representing the souls of the community's dearly departed ancestors.

ד

Serab el Khadem
Sinai, Proto-Canaanite
1500 BCE

Proto-Canaanite
13th–12th BCE

Ahiram Sarcophagus
Phoenician
1000 BCE

Gezer Calendar
Hebrew
End of 10th century BCE

Mesha Stete
Hebrew Script
Mid 9th century BCE

Kilamu Inscription
Phoenician last third
of 9th century BCE

Siloam Inscription
Hebrew
Late 8th century BCE

Hebrew Seals
7th century BCE

Hebrew Ostraca
Arad
Early 6th century BCE

Elephantine Papyrus
Aramaic
Late 5th century BCE

Leviticus Scroll, Qumran
Paleo-Hebrew
Late 2nd century BCE

Samaritan Manuscript
13th century BCE

Isaiah Scroll I Qumran
Square Hebrew Script
Late 2nd century BCE

Classical Greek Script

Latin Script

Nabataean Script
1st century BCE

Classical
Arabic Script

The ancient Babylonians and Persians began their New Year in the spring. The ancient Egyptians began their New Year in the summer when the waters of the Nile river started to rise. The ancient Romans began their New Year in the winter.

The Jews begin their New Year in the autumn when the entire harvest of the fields was gathered and the earth gets dry in the heat, waiting for the first rain, believing that the New Year should begin with a new crop.

The Shofar, the ram's horn, used in religious ceremonies, blows sadness, awe, and fear into our hearts.

We greet our new year with sadness and a broken heart, and not with joy like the rest of the nations of the world.

The New Year Days of Awe end with Yom Kippur, also a fast day, known as Yom-Hatruah, the day of blowing the ram's horn.

יום ־ כיפור
Hebrew—Yom Kippur
Yiddish—Yom Kipper

Yom Kippur is the holiest day of the year, when Jews cleanse themselves of sin. When sins are forgiven, they feel spiritually redeemed. The blowing of the Shofar reminds us of the day we were given the Torah on Mt. Sinai, and with it we are thankful to God for being forgiven.

It is also said that we are to ask forgiveness not only of God but of the ones we may have insulted or caused harm to.

This is considered the day when all Jews are judged in heaven for the year ahead, some for life and some for death, some for health and some for sickness, some for poverty and some for riches.

שׁ Shin

שׁ Shin   שׂ Sin

Numerical Value of 300

Shin—Represents the sound Sh

Sin—Represents the sound S

Pictorial representation of a tooth.

It has three branches on top of it.

The word *Shaddai* represents
one of the 72 names of God.

Moses and the burning bush: "I am the Lord. I appeared to Abraham, to Isaac, and to Jacob as God Almighty, but by my name the Lord (YHWH) I did not make myself known to them."

According to Exodus 6:2–3, El Shaddai is the name by which God was known to Abraham, Isaac, and Jacob. The term may be recognized in most English Bibles as "God Almighty." The name Shaddai (Hebrew—שַׁדַּי) is also used as a name of God later in the Book of Job.

A Theory

One theory about the term is that *Shaddai* is a derivation of the *Akkadian shadû* (mountain) or *shaddû`a* (mountain-dweller), one of the names of the Amorite god Amurru. Shaddai was also a late Bronze Age Amorite city on the banks of the Euphrates river, in northern Syria. In this theory, El Shaddai is seen as inhabiting a mythical holy mountain, as well as the sacred high places of early Israelite religion such as Bethel, Mount Carmel, and others. He was once identical with the Hebrew God, who later came to be identified with Yahweh.

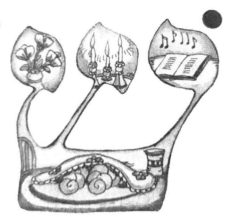

The word שקר (sheker) signifies "falsehood."

The author of the Zohar (the Book of Splendor), Moses ben Shemtov de Leon, makes an analogy between the letter Bet in the word *Breyshit* בראשית (in the beginning) and the Shin in שיר השירים, *Shir Hashirim*, Song of Songs.

Consequently the Shin conceals within its walls the mysteries of the Song of Songs, just as the letter Bet conceals the mysteries of creation.

———◁•▷———

שבת
Hebrew—*Shabbat*
Yiddish—*Shabbes*
Sabbath

It is customary to eat onions on the Sabbath. Onions are known to have seven layers of skin, symbolizing the seven days of the week. As it is said: "It is not that the Jews kept the Sabbath, as much as the Sabbath kept the Jews.

שלום
Hebrew—*Shalom*
Yiddish—*Sholem*
Peace

It is said that it's better to have a bad peace rather than a good war.

שדכן
Hebrew—*Shadkhan*
Yiddish—*Shadkhen*
A Matchmaker

A Bridal Custom

It was customary to cover a bride's hair with honey for a sweet life.

Among the Jews in Lithuania, before a wedding, a "throne" was prepared for the bride, made out of a big piece of dough. A pillow was placed on the dough, covered with a blanket, and the bride sat on it.

This was done in the hope that when the time comes, the bride's womb would rise like the dough, bringing her many babies.

In case of a difficult delivery, a string was attached from the foot of the bed and carried all the way to the Seyfer Toyreh, the Holy Torah scrolls, in the synagogue.

If that didn't help, all clothing drawers in the home were opened, all garments unbuttoned, all ties untied; and if that didn't help, the entire household would cry along in pain until the sound of the baby's crying was heard.

The Legend of a Wicked Nobleman

The story is told about a wicked Polish nobleman who came into a town where Jews lived and wanted to know the name of the town. So he ventured into a synagogue and, seeing a Jew praying, asked him: "What is this town called?"

But the man refused to stop his prayers to answer. So the wicked nobleman asked again and again while the Jew refused to interrupt his prayer. The nobleman lost his temper and punched the man in his jaw.

The Jew realized that the nobleman had broken his tooth, and he cried out: "Sebre-Shin" You broke my tooth…

The nobleman said: "Now you tell me that the town is called Shebreshin. You could have told it to me when I asked you the first time."

And from then on, the town in Poland was called Shebreshin.

שכן

Shokhn

Neighbor

The Baal Shem Tov and His Neighbor (Folklore)

The Baal Shem Tov—Reb Yisroel of Mezritch (1700–1760)—the founder of the Hassidic movement, once wanted to know who his neighbor would be in the world to come. He pleaded with God to reveal the mystery to him, and God obliged.

When he found out the man's identity, he took a horse and buggy and off he went to find his neighbor in the world to come. He hoped to get acquainted and chat with him about the Holy Torah.

The Baal Shem Tov

He arrives in a small village, searches out the man's meager abode, opens the door, and sees a healthy, strong, and corpulent man without a beard or *payes* (sidelocks), gorging himself on food, paying little attention to the goings on around him.

The Baal Shem Tov was greatly surprised, thinking, *How could this good-for-nothing slob be my neighbor in Paradise?*

He waited for quite a long time for the bloated man to stop eating, and when he finally did, the Baal Shem Tov asked him: "Please tell me, *Reb Yid* (Mister), why are you eating so much?"

The man confided in him: "My father was a short, skinny little Jew who could hardly catch his breath. When the *kossacks* came into our town, ready to set a pogrom on us Jews, they caught my father, tied him to a tree, and set him on fire. Within a split of a second, my father was scorched and died, that's how little my father was.

"And when I witnessed this, I promised myself that I would not burn as easily. I will burn with a fire that will be seen from one side of the world to the other, Rebbe. That is the reason I eat so much."

שלום־עליכם
Hebrew—*Shalom Aleikhem*
Yiddish—*Sholem Aleichem*
Traditional greeting: *Peace Be Upon You.*
A classic Yiddish writer

Sholem ben Menakhem Nokhem Rabinowitz, pen name Sholem Aleichem, was born in Pereyaslev, the Ukraine, in 1859 and died in New York in 1916. One hundred thousand people followed his funeral. *Fiddler on the Roof* is based on his "Tevye the Dairyman" stories.

Sholem Aleichem,
classic Yiddish writer

EQUALITY FOR ALL
by Sholem Aleichem

When God banished Adam and Eve from the Garden of Eden, they began to multiply and fill the earth for generations. Their offspring decided the world was too crowded. They couldn't come to terms with the inheritance that they had received from their great, great, great grandparents. They settled throughout the entire world, each with his language, each with his faith, forgetting their common lineage, and they began declaring war on each other.

The result was a great "mish-mash" mixture with different customs and traditions, with different classes of people—both masters and slaves, servants and proprietors, bosses and workers, and, in time, people believed that this was how the world was meant to be.

In time, the world got smarter and people began to ask: "Why do some have it all and we have nothing?"

Then humanity went on a killing spree and spilled barrels of blood and cried buckets of tears. When they realized that all people would disappear and the world would be destroyed, a pleading letter was proposed to God Almighty:

"Please straighten out the world and make peace on Earth."

But where could they find someone who could compose such a letter, someone whom God respects? They found such a man among the little Red Jews who lived on the other side of the River Sambatyon.*

He was articulate and he knew the Biblical holy tongue.

He began with a blessing:

Sholem Aleichem's funeral on May 15, 1916, attracted more than 150,000 mourners.

"Dear Enlightener, our great God that created a perfect world, which has but one fault. There is no equality among people. Some have all the land, the food and the money and others have nothing. There is one fellow in America by the name of Rockefeller who is worth billions and earns more than two hundred million dollars a year, which is as good as seven hundred thousand Ruble a day, while his workers slave away sixteen hours every day and have to support a wife and six hungry children. How many Rockefellers, Vanderbilts, and Rothschilds there are in the world, so we plead with you, Dear God, in the name of all the poor people, to do a righteous accounting, cash in all the money in the world and divide it among the poor people equally, there will be no more hatred, jealousy, and bloodshed, and peace will descend upon the world."

Everyone, except the wealthiest, signed the letter, and it was sent off to the Celestial Court of Justice.

God payed attention and decided to act. He collected all the money in the world and created peace among men, with no hatred and no jealousy.

On the fourth day of Peace on Earth a fiery tablet was seen in the heavens with fiery numbers overhead illuminating this celestial equation:

$$15,000,000,000,000 : 1,500,000,000 = 10,000$$

---

*Legendary Sambatyon River, impossible to cross because it spews rocks all week long, but on the Sabbath it rests when Jews are forbidden to cross. On the other side of the river presumably live the Ten Lost Jewish Tribes.

15 trillion dollars divided by 1.5 billion people equals ten thousand dollars.

People realized that this was a true Heavenly accounting and that each person on the planet was worth ten thousand dollars.

The entire Earth celebrated and all of humankind was joyful. The poor people in the world were ecstatic and everyone lined up to get their ten thousand dollars. No one took more and no one took less and they all went home happy singing their favorite songs.

They all thanked the Holy One for his honesty and righteousness, for his grace and his mercy, which he finally shared with the sinful human race that He redeemed from great tragedies. He certainly wouldn't allow the world to be destroyed over such an insignificant thing as money. And everyone lived happily ever after.

<hr />

> שרעק
> Yiddish—*Shrek*
> Fear

SHREK
by Fishl Bimko

A plague broke out and the human destruction was great, it tore mothers from children and grooms from brides.

The plague hadn't reached the town where this Rabbi resided, a righteous man that deluded himself into believing that he would not allow the plague to enter his town.

There were people that believed him while others doubted his ability to stop the plague.

The Rabbi did everything, including blowing the ram's horn— the Shofar, lighting candles on the holy graves of the rabbi's tombs in the cemetery.

All this helped for a while. The Rabbi stood like a giant

Yiddish writer
Fishl Bimko

protecting his town, until the bad news started to trickle in that the plague was approaching the town.

The town quivered and shivered with fear, so the Rabbi decided to step outside the border of his town. It was there that he would have his discourse with God, Blessed be He.

While he was in the midst of his debate with God, he saw the Angel of Death approaching.

He grabbed him by the arm and called out: "Where do you think you are going?"

"I'm going into town!" the Angel of Death replied.

The Rabbi cried out: "I won't let you in!"

The Angel of Death responded: "I have orders from someone more powerful than you."

The Rabbi stood strong and powerful: "I am more revered and mightier than you."

The Angel of Death took out a document with thirteen names. "Stand aside," he said. "I have to take these thirteen souls with me."

The Rabbi thought for a moment. Thirteen people? Maybe he shouldn't be opposed to the Celestial Body—the Court of Justice in Heaven—and create a horrible commotion.

He relented, warning the Angel of Death: "Alright, I'll let you in, but you must swear that you will take only the thirteen on your list."

The Angel of Death replied: "I will only take those on my list!"

When the Rabbi reached the town he heard the wailing from afar.

People were yelling: "Help us, rabbi, people are dying like flies."

"How many graves have you dug already?" asked the Rabbi.

"Seven!" He was told.

ש	
ص	Serab el Khadem Sinai, Proto-Canaanite 1500 BCE
Ƹ	Proto-Canaanite 13th–12th BCE
ᔑ	Ahiram Sarcophagus Phoenician 1000 BCE
ᘯ	Gezer Calendar Hebrew End of 10th century BCE
ᗯ	Mesha Stete Hebrew Script Mid 9th century BCE
ᗺ	Kilamu Inscription Phoenician last third of 9th century BCE
ᗲ	Siloam Inscription Hebrew Late 8th century BCE
ᗄᐧ	Hebrew Seals 7th century BCE
ᘉ	Hebrew Ostraca Arad Early 6th century BCE
ᘃ	Elephantine Papyrus Aramaic Late 5th century BCE
ᘸ	Leviticus Scroll, Qumran Paleo-Hebrew Late 2nd century BCE
ᴡ	Samaritan Manuscript 13th century BCE
ע	Isaiah Scroll I Qumran Square Hebrew Script Late 2nd century BCE
Σ	Classical Greek Script
S	Latin Script
⨍	Nabataean Script 1st century BCE
ش	Classical Arabic Script

"Seven?" shouts the rabbi.

The people kept counting: "Eight! Nine! Ten! Eleven! Twelve! Thirteen!"

The Rabbi shouted: "Stop! That's enough!"

The people took a deep breath.

Suddenly the Rabbi heard: "Fourteen. Reb Mendele is also gone!"

The Rabbi ran into the town market searching for the Angel of Death.

"The last one was not on your list, you murderer. You were supposed to take only thirteen, a promise is a promise. Where is God?"

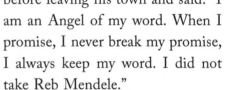

The Angel of Death turned to the Rabbi before leaving his town and said: "I am an Angel of my word. When I promise, I never break my promise, I always keep my word. I did not take Reb Mendele."

"Why is he dead then?" shouts the Rabbi hopelessly.

"You see!" shouts the Angel of Death. "Reb Mendele was so fearful that he died of 'Shrek.'"

Surviving Hatred—A True Holocaust Story

Josef Katz, a young Jew in the Carpathian mountains during the war, was given money by his father to buy a nice suit in the hope that the Nazis would overlook the fact that he was a Jew.

Unwittingly, he bought a suit that belonged to the Hitler Youth movement and the Nazis who surrounded him believed that he was one of them. In spite of the fact that he looked Jewish, he was given a rifle and sent to be a guard at a Nazi camp in Austria.

This is how he survived the hatred of the Jews in Europe.

ת Saf

ת Taf ת Saf

Numeric Value of 400

Hebrew—Taf, Saf   Yiddish—Tof, Sof

The End

The last letter of the Jewish Alphabet

Saf literally means "sign and mark." It also symbolizes the end of things, namely Death.

The name Taf is based on a Talmudic passage in Ezekiel, where the Lord made Ezekiel go through the city of Jerusalem and make a Taf sign on the foreheads of those who cried out in horror upon seeing the devastation of the Temple.

The Taf on the foreheads of the צדיקים—*Tsadikim*, the righteous—meant that they knew the entire Torah from Alef to Taf.

תורה

Hebrew—*Torah*

Yiddish—*Toyre*

Known as Khumash or Khumesh, the Jewish Bible, The Five Books of Moses, the *Tanakh* that stands for *Torah* (Knowledge), *Neviyim* (Prophets), and *Ktuvim* (Writings).

Rabbi Akiva once asked: "Why is the little leg of the letter Taf bent?"

The answer lies in the definition of the word תורה—Torah—itself. It starts with the letter Taf, meaning that whoever wants to learn the Torah must bend their knee and sit down to study.

The Fate of the Alef-Bet

The masters of the Kabbalah, the mystics, add that the letter Taf represents the sacred boundary to a mysterious sea of fantastic ideas, streaming within the walls of the letter. The Taf is their shore and nothing exists beyond it. Some mystics were courageous enough to go a step further and ponder upon the possibility of a 24th (?) letter, which would be the most mysterious of them all.

The mystics conclude that at the end of days, the worlds will ascend and slowly dissolve one onto the other, the lower onto the higher.

The same fate awaits the letters of the Alef-Bet, the Torah, sacred text, even the sacred letters יהוה Yud Hey Vav Heh, signifying God's name.

Everything will dissolve and become one with the cosmos and return to the state that it was on the very eve of creation. It will dissolve into the one and only primordial letter ת—Taf.

תלמוד

Hebrew—*Talmud*
The Biblical Commentaries

A vast collection of the civil and religious laws of the Jewish faith, the Talmud contains extensive scholarly debates, discussions of law, ethics, values, and traditions. There is a Talmudic precept that says:

"There are certain sounds that reach from one end of the world to the other, among them are sunset, space, the sounds of nations, the sound of the soul that frees itself of the body, and the sound of a woman in labor."

There is a Talmud *Bavli,* composed in Babylonia in Aramaic and a Talmud *Yerushalmi,* composed in Jerusalem in the year 350 CE.

Talmud means learning. The *Mishnah* is the first section of the Talmud, containing post-biblical laws and rabbinic commentaries, dating from the year 200 CE.

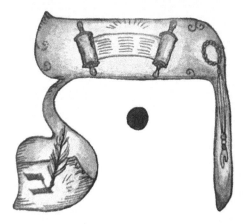

The Talmud is a document that contains our recorded history, philosophy, psychology, astronomy, mathematics, metaphysics, medicine, art, and literature. It is also a depository of wisdom, questions and answers that are to this day dispensed throughout the ages for all generations.

A Threat to Jewish Life

While Jews were persecuted throughout history, they needed to retain their political, national, religious, economic, social, and cultural well-being.

Under the constant Roman and Greek yokes and oppressions at a time when the old generation lived under the spell of the old way of life and memories of a stable Jewish life, and what was lost while the life of the young generation hung on a scale between Judaism and Secularism, while Rome conquered the world.

With one exception, all these ruling states had come across a stubborn, headstrong people, threatening their physical and spiritual people, and when the Romans began threatening the Jews by forbidding practice of their religion, that is when Rabbi Akiva was convinced that the redemption was near and began supporting Bar Kokhba, who organized a revolt against the Romans and their Greek culture, which began to penetrate every nuance of Jewish existence in the land of Judah, influencing our language, way of dress, customs, and behavior. This secular Greek-Roman culture slowly began to threaten our Jewish life.

The Talmud tells of four rabbis who began the search into secularism, namely four Talmud scholars who undertook to look into Greek philosophy, their poetry and their art; they were out to taste the forbidden fruit, the wisdom of the Greeks.

A walk through the Orchard of Jewish Knowledge, which deals with the four rabbis of the first two centuries CE whose teachings are included in the Mishnah, which is the first section of the Talmud, containing post-biblical laws and rabbinic commentaries.

One of them was Rabbi Azay, the second was Rabbi ben Zuma, the third Elisha ben Abuya, and the fourth Rabbi Akiva. Notice that the third, Elisha ben Abuya was not called rabbi: the reason, he betrayed his religious beliefs. The Talmud calls him "Akher" or "Ish Akher," the other, he who betrayed.

The Talmud says that as far as Rabbi Shimon ben Azay is concerned, he looked into the secular writings and died. How is it possible to look into the forbidden books and die? The answer is that before the eyes of Rabbi Shimon ben Azay there was suddenly revealed a strange and foreign world with a different view that he didn't know how to deal with.

Rabbi Shimon ben Zoma, a student of Rabbi Yehoshua, was a great Torah scholar and a great orator; his great wisdom was known throughout the land and his people, but the non Jews around him plagiarized his wisdom, stole his teachings, and called them as their own. Rabbi Shimon ben Zoma made famous such wisdom as:

Who is the wise man? He who learns from every man.

Who is a hero? He who can overcome his own temptations.

Who is rich? He who is happy with his lot.

Who is the honorable man? He who honors others.

ת	
†	Serab el Khadem Sinai, Proto-Canaanite 1500 BCE
╋	Proto-Canaanite 13th–12th BCE
†	Ahiram Sarcophagus Phoenician 1000 BCE
⊀	Gezer Calendar Hebrew End of 10th century BCE
×	Mesha Stete Hebrew Script Mid 9th century BCE
ʈ	Kilamu Inscription Phoenician last third of 9th century BCE
×	Siloam Inscription Hebrew Late 8th century BCE
X	Hebrew Seals 7th century BCE
✕	Hebrew Ostraca Arad Early 6th century BCE
ɟ	Elephantine Papyrus Aramaic Late 5th century BCE
✗	Leviticus Scroll, Qumran Paleo-Hebrew Late 2nd century BCE
Ⲛ	Samaritan Manuscript 13th century BCE
ת	Isaiah Scroll I Qumran Square Hebrew Script Late 2nd century BCE
Τ	Classical Greek Script
T	Latin Script
ﬡ	Nabataean Script 1st century BCE
‫ت‬	Classical Arabic Script

Rabbi Akiva said:

"Love your neighbor as yourself.
That is the Foundation of the Torah."

Rabbi Akiva

תח ות"ט
1648–1649
Takh veTat

Takh veTat is known in Jewish history as a period of horrific massacres of Jews—Also known as Chmielnitzcki's Pogrom in the Ukraine, Podolya, East Galicia, parts of eastern Poland, and the north reaching Vilna in Lithuania. Over 300 Jewish communities were slaughtered by the Kossacks and the Turks. Approximately half a million Jews perished. Many Jews were taken into captivity by the Turks and sold on the slave markets. The Turkish Jews ransomed the Jewish slaves.

Story about the Baal Shem Tov, Master of His Good Name

I've chosen the following stories and vignettes as a beautiful bookend to the more formal entries in the book. Enjoy!

nce, the holy **Rebbe Baal Shem Tov**, the founder of Hassidism, decided to leave his hometown of Mezhibuzh in Eastern Europe and settle in the land of Israel. So he took along his daughter Odl and his scribe, Reb Hirsh, and they proceeded on their journey. They traveled and traveled until they reached Konstantinopol, the Capital of Turkey. There he decided to hire a boat and travel to the Holy Land.

In the midst of their journey, a big storm broke out and all three of them were carried away to unknown places.

"Rebbe!" cried out Reb Hirsh the scribe, "Do something! Or else we are all going to perish here!"

So the Baal Shem Tov said a prayer, and they landed on an unfamiliar island. But Reb Hirsh was full of fear when he approached the Baal Shem Tov with trepidation: "Rebbe! All you have to say is a couple of sacred words, and we'll get out alive."

Said the Baal Shem Tov: "In my fear I have forgotten everything, I can't even remember a couple of words from our Holy Torah."

"But I have also forgotten everything," said Reb Hirsh. "All I remember is our Alef-Beyz, our alphabet."

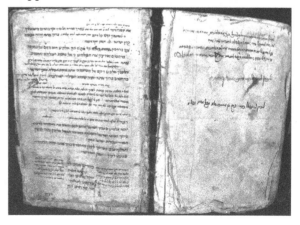

"How wonderful!" cried out the Baal Shem Tov. "So let's start with our Alef-Beyz, our alphabet."

So Reb Hirsh began reciting: "Alef, Beyz, Giml, Daled," while the Baal Shem Tov caught the spirit and went on, "Hey, Vav, Zayin, Khes, Tes," … and so on….

Suddenly he remembered it all! At this point he understood that he was not yet expected up in Heaven—he had many more years left to guide his Hassidic flock, and as frustrated as he was, he, his daughter Odl, and his scribe, Reb Hirsh, had to return to their shtetl Medzhibuzh and proceed with his assigned purpose in life, which was the study of the Torah and the spread of Hassidism.

Yiddish Proverb

צוויי טויזנט יאָר האָבן ייִדן געטרוימט וועגן
אַן אייגן לאַנד און מיך האָט עס געדאַרפֿט טרעפֿן

Tzvey toyznt yor hobn Yidn getroymt veygn
An eygn land un mikh hot es gedarft trefn

Meaning: For two thousand years,
Jews dreamt of a land of their own,
and it had to happen to me!

The Israelis greet the new immigrant in Hebrew with:

ברוך השם אתה בארץ
Barukh Hashem ata baaretz

Meaning: "Bless God that you are in our land."

Aretz represents land, ground, and down under, which the new immigrant repeats in Yiddish:

אוי בין איך אין דר׳ערד. איך בין גוט און טיף אין דר׳ערד
Oy bin ikh in d'rerd. Ikh bin git un tif in d'rerd

Meaning: "Wow, I am deep in the ground." In other words: "Oh boy, I am in the dumps!"

Folk Religion

Alongside the formal religion, we had a folk-religion, practices which were not always approved of by the religious establishment; still it enjoyed its popularity.

> אָפּשפּרעכערקעס
> *Opshprekherkes*
> Dispellers of the Evil Eye

Practically every Jewish small town and village in the Ukraine had its "Dispellers," to whom the pregnant women would go, especially when they were about to bear their first child.

The old women knew whether the baby would be a boy or a girl using non-conventional remedies like herbs, cuppings (*Bankes*), and leeches.

They also knew how to exorcise a *Dybbuk*, an evil spirit or soul of a dead person residing in the body of a living individual, which can only be expelled by "magical" means. The Dispellers could also foretell the future.

"I have always thought that every woman should marry, but no man!"
—Benjamin Disraeli (1804–1884), Jewish British Statesman

From the Memoirs of Glikl Hamel

Glikl Hamel (German—Gluckel von Hameln) was born in 1646 in Hamburg, Germany, and lived in the small town of Hameln.

Glikl Hamel

Glikl, married at fourteen, was a mother of ten who conducted a successful business after her husband's premature death. She wrote her memoirs in old Yid-dish in order to acquaint her children with their family history. In her memoir, she describes the tragic events of the Black Plague, as well as the messianic debacle of Shabtai Zvi, the false Messiah. Her writings are permeated with sayings and quotations from various biblical and Midrashic sources. She represented the unique blend of pious devotion and worldliness.

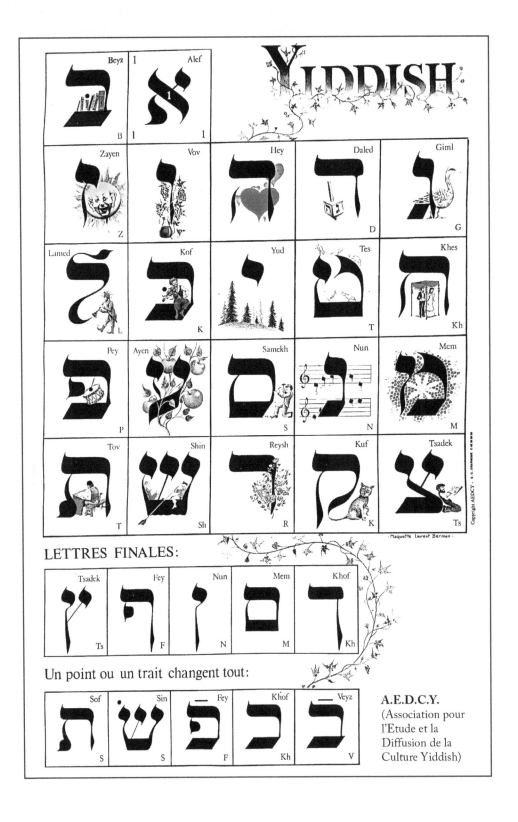

Name	Paleo-Hebrew	Block	Samaritan	Phonetic value (Pre-Exilic)[53][54] (IPA)
Aleph	⩵	א	𐤀	[ʔ], ∅
Beth	𐤁	ב	𐤁	[b], β
Gimel	𐤂	ג	𐤂	[g], ɣ
Daleth	◁	ד	𐤃	[d], ð
He	𐤄	ה	𐤄	[h], ∅
Waw	𐤅	ו	𐤅	[w], ∅
Zayin	I	ז	𐤆	[z]
Heth	𐤇	ח	𐤇	[ħ], [χ][55][56]
Teth	⊕	ט	♡	[tˤ][55][56]
Yodh	𐤉	י	𐤉	[j], ∅
Kaph	𐤊	כ, ך	𐤊	[k], x
Lamedh	𐤋	ל	𐤋	[l]
Mem	𐤌	מ, ם	𐤌	[m]
Nun	𐤍	נ, ן	𐤍	[n]
Samekh	≢	ס	𐤎	[s]
Ayin	O	ע	𐤏	[ʕ], [ʁ][55][56]
Pe	𐤐	פ, ף	𐤐	[p], ɸ
Sadhe	𐤑	צ, ץ	𐤑	[sˤ][55][56]
Qoph	𐤒	ק	𐤒	[q] or [kˤ][55][56]
Resh	𐤓	ר	𐤓	[r]
Shin	W	ש	ш	[ʃ], [ɬ][55][56]
Taw	✗	ת	𐤕	[t], θ

Acknowledgments

I would like to acknowledge the following people who supported and inspired me throughout my life:

My Father, Chaim Schmulewitz, writer, satirist and humorist.

My husband, Mendl Hoffman, who insisted I write a column in the *Yiddish Forward*, and encouraged me to write plays, do my post graduate studies at Columbia University, and accept their position of Yiddish Professor where I taught for 25 years. He also encouraged me to teach Yiddish for several summers at Oxford University as well as at the University of Vilnius in Lithuania.

My son Avrum (Avi) Hoffman, who is my co-founder of the Yiddishkayt Initiative, and who is extremely helpful in preparing my books for publishing as well as developing my many plays, programs, and presentations that deal with Yiddish language and culture that we present around the world.

My loving son Ben Hoffman, who tends to my welfare.

Mr. David Mattis, who invited me to write weekly articles in the *Yiddish Forward*.

Mrs. Sore Rukhl Schaechter Viswanath, the current editor of the *Yiddish Forward*, who has remained true to her profession.

My beloved Yiddish, teacher Chaim Kazdan, at both the Workmen's Circle Yiddish Mitlshul and the Jewish Teachers Seminary

Mr. Yankev Levin, my teacher at the Workmen's Circle Mitlshul, who invited me to be a counselor at his Yiddish Summer Colony in Newburgh, New York.

Dr. Phillip Friedman, historian and Director of the Jewish Teachers Seminary, who taught us Jewish History.

Prof. Yitskhak Kharlash, literature teacher, who taught and inspired us to read books by world famous writers

Prof. Hasya Kuperman, New School for Social Studies, where I won the first prize in 1956 for my literary essay "The difference between I.L. Peretz's "Bontche Shweig" and Isaac Bashevis-Singer's "Gimpl Tam."

The Jewish Teacher's Seminary, which proclaimed a literary contest of which I was the winner of the $350 First Prize for my Literary Essay entitled "What Does My Judaism Consist of?"

I received my second B.A. at the University of Miami, Florida in 1979. Among my teachers were:

Dr. Yehuda Shamir, with whom I studied Talmud, Kabbalah, and Yiddish at Oxford University in England; Dr. Dovid Katz, who invited me to teach Yiddish at Oxford University in England, as well as at the University of Vilnius in Lithuania.

I will forever be grateful to Professor Rakhmiel Peltz, who invited me to teach Yiddish and Yiddish Culture at Columbia University, where I wound up teaching for 25 years.

Among my other professors were:

Prof. Jack Kugelmass at Columbia University, who inspired me in my studies and suggested that I turn my Master's Thesis into a Ph.D.

Professor Yitzhak Niborsky at The Sorbonne University in Paris, whom I befriended at Oxford University and who counseled me not to be afraid of Yiddish grammar.

My co-writer and wonderful friend, Rena Borow.

My dear friend Aviva Astrinsky, former Chief Librarian of Yivo Institute of Jewish Research, who has helped me significantly with my research

My dearest friend and theatrical mentor, Joseph Papp, born Yosele Papirowsky, world-famous impresario and founder of the New York Shakespeare Festival/Public Theater. He was the first one to produce our Yiddish/English musical "Songs of Paradise," and with whom I spent several years preparing the materials for the annual YIVO Benefits. Joseph Papp invited Broadway and Hollywood stars to participate in these events and I was honored to meet such great luminaries of stage and screen.

I am in great awe of my beloved friend Gail Merrifield Papp, herself a talented writer and widowed spouse of Joseph Papp.

Among other stars that came my way:

Leonard Nimoy, Yiddish-speaking star of *Star Trek,* for his invaluable friendship; Theodore Bikel and Fyvush Finkel, who starred in my Yiddish translation of Neil Simon's *The Sunshine Boys* at the Symphony Space in New York.

My gratitude is also extended to:

Sam Norich, former Executive Director of YIVO Institute for Jewish Research, for being the first executive to acknowledge and partner with the Joseph Papp Yiddish Theater and Leo Greenboym, YIVO archivist, for his great help in my research.

My deep gratitude goes to:

William Dellinger and Peggy Quinsenbery at Columbia University, for becoming dear friends and supporters during the difficult moments at Columbia University, and who extended a helping hand in acquiring my computers and printers for years.

My gratitude is extended to my longtime friends, among them:

My very best friend in New York, Bella Schaechter-Gottesman, artist, poet and song-writer.

Moishe Goldstein, Director of the Sholem Aleichem Shul 21, Yiddish School in the Bronx, where I began my teaching career as a kindergarten teacher.

My friend Malke Gottlieb, pianist and accompanist for my early plays.

Binyumin Schaechter, talented composer and accompanist for several of my plays.

Dr. Ruth Snopkowsky of Munich and Regensburg, who first brought my play *A Rendezvous with God* to Germany.

Mira Rafalowitz, who brought our play, Songs of Paradise, to the annual Yiddish Festival in Amsterdam, Holland, after which both plays appeared in Warsaw, Poland; Zurich, Switzerland; and Israel.

Special acknowledgement to:

Bryna Wasserman and The Dora Wasserman Yiddish Theater of Montreal, Canada, for staging my plays *Hard to be a Jew* (adapted into a musical from Sholem Aleichem), my Yiddish translations of Neil Simon's *The Sunshine Boys,* Mel Brooks' *The Producers,* and my adaptation of Ansky's *The Dybbuk.*

Sue Lawless at Queens Theater in the Park for producing my play *Noble Laureate.*

My great appreciation for Tsipora Spaizman, former director of The National Yiddish Theatre–Folksbiene which presented my plays *Hard to Be a Jew, The Ludmirer Moyd,* and *Songs of Paradise.*

The National Yiddish Theatre of Israel, Yiddishpiel, for presenting *Songs of Paradise* and my Yiddish translation of Neil Simon's *The Sunshine Boys* and *The Odd Couple,* which received the highest prize for Israeli Theatre.

I take great pleasure in acknowledging:

Cornelia (Krayndl) Martyn, my former student at Columbia University, who is now Professor of Yiddish at Potsdam University, Germany.

Dr. Kalmen Weiser, my former student at Columbia University, who is now History Professor at the University of Toronto, Canada.

Kolya Baradulin, who arrived from Birobidzhan, in the former Soviet Union, and joined my Yiddish class at Columbia University. Today, he is a Director and Yiddish teacher at the Workmen's Circle. He is also the organizer of the Yiddish Program at the Circle Lodge in Hopewell Junction, New York.

I should like to extend my very warmest admiration and love to Feygele (Florence) and Muniele (Michael) Edelstein, my childhood friends and supporters, who are the Founding Sponsors of the Yiddishkayt Initiative and who produced my Yiddish radio show on WEVD in New York with the best Yiddish actors of the day; among them Eleanor Reissa, Avi Hoffman, Michael Alpert, Susan Katchko, Suzanne Toren, and musical director Malke Gottlieb.

I would also like to extend my warmest regards to my new friends at the Writer's Cafe at the Parkland Library in Florida and Gary & Carol Rosenberg, The Book Couple, for their indispensable support in making my books possible.

About the Author

Miriam Hoffman earned her first baccalaureate (B.A.) in 1957 from the Jewish Teachers Seminary in New York, which was accepted at the New School for Social Research in New York in 1981, upon her return from a decade living in Israel. In 1982, she earned her second B.A. at the University of Miami.

In 1982, Miriam was accepted at Columbia University of New York and majored in Yiddish folklore and literature, where she did all her graduate work. Today she is Professor of Yiddish language, literature, Jewish culture, Yiddish humor, classical and minor Yiddish writers, and a course called 20th Century Yiddish Literature and Film. She taught at Columbia University from 1992 to 2015.

Miriam is the author of *A Breed Apart: Reflections of a Young Refugee,* the highly personal and historic account of the author's life that brings to light the oppression of the Soviet regime, the five-year history of the Displaced Persons Refugee Camps (DP camps) in Germany from 1946 to 1951, the struggles of post–World War II anti-Semitism, and her coming of age in America.

She has also written a Yiddish textbook called *Key to Yiddish,* which includes scholarly research, conversation, folklore, folktales, songs, and literary works by the most acclaimed Yiddish writers and poets. *Key to Yiddish* also contains humorous illustrations that appeared in the Yiddish magazine *Der Groyser Kundas,* in print from 1911 to 1929.

The Author Graduating Workmen's Circle Mitlshul (2nd row, 1st from left)

The very last chapter in *Key to Yiddish* includes Miriam's successful play called *The Maiden of Ludmir,* which deals with the first female Orthodox rabbi in the Ukraine of 1805–1892. *The Maiden of Ludmir* was performed at the Folksbiene Theater. *Key to Yiddish* is now used in many universities all over the world.

Miriam is also a successful Yiddish playwright. She has written many plays including *Reflections of a Lost Poet,* which deals with the life and works of the most beloved Yiddish poet Itzik Manger and which is still being performed today both in the United States and Israel and, as of 2016, is being staged in Bucharest, Romania.

Miriam has written several plays with Rena Borow, among them the play *Noble Laureate.* Isaac Bashevis-Singer was the Nobel Laureate for Literature in 1978, and the play is named after a since-corrected misspelling on his tombstone. The play tells of Isaac Bashevis-Singer's battle with dementia in the declining years of his life in Miami Beach, Florida. It was performed at the Queens Theater in the Park in New York City.

Miriam's plays were also staged at the Folksbiene National Yiddish Theater of New York, The Yiddish Theatre of Saidye Bronfman, the Centre for the Arts in Montreal, Canada, and the Yiddishpiel Theater in Israel. Miriam is the recipient of the Israeli Tony Award for her Yiddish translation of Neil Simon's *The Sunshine Boys.* Her Yiddish translation of Mel Brooks's *The Producers* was performed to great acclaim in 2016. It ran for several months to sold-out houses at the Dora Wasserman Yiddish Theater and the Alvin Siegel Center in Montreal, Canada.

Miriam is also a known Yiddish journalist and worked as a feature writer for the *Yiddish Forward* from 1982 to today.

The years 2014–2015 saw Miriam's retirement from Columbia University after twenty-five years of dedicated work. Since then, she is still busy writing her column for the *Yiddish Forward,* and working on a new Yiddish play called *Shiklgruber and Dzugashvili,* the original names of Hitler and Stalin, a musical comedy in two acts. Miriam still lectures on the topic of "Yiddish in Living Color."

OTHER BOOKS BY PROFESSOR MIRIAM HOFFMAN

KEY TO YIDDISH

Key to Yiddish aims to introduce the student to the fundamentals of Yiddish language and culture.

It contains idiomatic constructions, dialogue, selected readings, exercises and worksheets, all geared to welcome the student to the world of Yiddish, its history, tradition, customs, rituals, songs, and holiday celebrations.

A BREED APART: REFLECTIONS OF A YOUNG REFUGEE

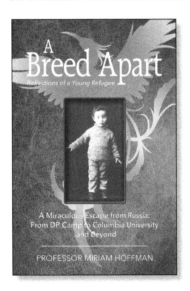

A Remarkable Historical Journey and Legacy

From Siberia to Columbia University, this epic tale of war and survival is seen through the eyes of a young Miriam Hoffman and her father, Chaim Schmulewitz, a well-respected columnist of the Yiddish press *Undzerweg.*

Highly personal and historic, *A Breed Apart* brings to light the oppression of the Soviet regime, the Displaced Persons Refugee Camps (DP camps) in Germany from 1946–51, the struggles of post–World War II anti-Semitism, and the author's coming of age in America.

AVAILABLE ON AMAZON.COM

CPSIA information can be obtained
at www.ICGtesting.com
Printed in the USA
BVHW021421110122
625987BV00007B/475

9 780999 336526